THE PLYMOUTH & DARTMOOR
and
THE LEE MOOR TRAMWAY

by
Eric R. Shepherd

ARK PUBLICATIONS (RAILWAYS)

First published in 1997 by ARK PUBLICATIONS (RAILWAYS), an imprint of
FOREST PUBLISHING, Woodstock, Liverton, Newton Abbot, Devon TQ12 6JJ

Copyright © Eric R. Shepherd 1997

All rights reserved. No part of this book may be reproduced or transmitted in any form or by any means, electronic or mechanical, including photocopying, recording or by any information storage or retrieval system, without written permission from the copyright holder.

British Library Cataloguing in Publication Data
A catalogue record for this book is available from the British Library
ISBN 1-873029-06-3

A loaded train crossing the GWR main line at Laira en route to Martin's Wharf in the 1920s.
F. H. C. Casbourn, courtesy of The Stephenson Locomotive Society

ARK PUBLICATIONS (RAILWAYS)
Editorial, design and layout by:
Mike Lang

Typeset by:
Carnaby Typesetting, Torquay, Devon TQ1 1EG

Printed and bound in Great Britain by:
BPC Wheatons Ltd, Exeter, Devon EX2 8RP

Cover photographs:

Front — (Top)   Part of The Plymouth & Dartmoor Railway across Yelverton Common, looking towards Princetown. Note the siding to the right, which is laid with granite rather than iron rails.
Courtesy of The Railway Magazine

(Lower)   A horse-drawn train to Torycombe approaching the sharp curve leading to the bridge over the River Plym in the 1920s.
F. H. C. Casbourn, courtesy of The Stephenson Locomotive Society

Back –   A horse-drawn train passing Laira GWR sidings in the 1920s.
F. H. C. Casbourn, courtesy of The Stephenson Locomotive Society

CONTENTS

	Page
Introduction	5
The Routes Described	7
The Plymouth & Dartmoor Railway and The Lee Moor Tramway – A Short History	47
The Plymouth & Dartmoor Railway – Rolling Stock	59
The Lee Moor Tramway – Rolling Stock	60
Engineering and Operating Data	64
The Lee Moor Tramway Preservation Society	66
The Remains of the Routes in 1996	76
The Granite Quarries of Walkhampton Common	107
Appendices	112
Bibliography	115
The Author	116

ACKNOWLEDGEMENTS

I would like to offer my sincere thanks to all those people who have assisted with, and provided information for, the compilation of this book. I am especially indebted to Mr. R. Taylor, for allowing free access to his considerable records concerning the Lee Moor Tramway; to Mr. D. Tozer, for his company and advice during many field visits to the remains of the railway routes; to Miss M. Gloyne, for providing information concerning the railway in the Yelverton area; to the staff of the Local Studies Library in Plymouth, for their assistance, particularly with old editions of maps depicting the courses of the various lines; to Mrs. A. Nicholson, for her meticulous work in typing the manuscript; to Mr. R. Zaple, for so skilfully originating the sketch maps and diagrams.

Last, but by no means least, to my wife, Margaret, for her encouragement and patience over many months.

(Photographs are acknowledged individually except those taken by me)

Slatestone sleepers remaining on the Cann Quarry line, above Plym Bridge. The overgrown bed of the Cann Canal is on the right (11th September 1996).

INTRODUCTION

The County of Devon has a long history of maritime trading, and a considerable portion of that trade has passed over the quays at Plymouth, in the south-western corner of the county. For many years the commodities handled on those quays included materials which had been brought down from the surrounding countryside on a system of railway lines, the first of which to be constructed was the main line of the Plymouth & Dartmoor Railway.

Opened in 1823, this line initially ran from Crabtree, on the eastern side of Plymouth, to granite quarries situated near Princetown, on Dartmoor, but was subsequently extended to Sutton Pool (at the southern end) and to the centre of Princetown (at the northern end) – bringing its total length up to no less than $25\frac{1}{2}$ miles! That was not all. By 1834 'branch' lines had been laid to Marsh Mills, to Cann Quarry in the Plym Valley and to Plympton, while later, in 1858, the system became larger still: the Lee Moor Tramway was connected to the Cann Quarry Railway at Plym Bridge for the purpose of serving the china clay industry at Lee Moor and Wotter, in the south-western corner of Dartmoor.

The track gauge of all these railways, which carried almost exclusively horse-drawn wagons, was 4 feet 6 inches. On the face of it, this was an unusual choice and one for which no obvious reason is apparent. It needs to be borne in mind, however, that the main-line railway had not reached Devon when the Plymouth & Dartmoor Railway was first conceived, so the possibility of other railway connections was not a consideration. Furthermore, the railways were initially constructed and operated principally for the carriage of minerals and general freight to, and from, one location, the quays at Plymouth.

In the pages that follow my aim is to describe by word and photograph when and where the lines of the Plymouth & Dartmoor Railway and the Lee Moor Tramway were operated, how they came into being, and what remains are to be seen in the present day of the various routes used. I must mention, however, that not all of these lines were in operation at the same time, so it is impossible to describe the system as a whole at any one period. It must be remembered, too, that in the years since 1823 there have been many housing, industrial and road-building changes, particularly in and around Plymouth, not to mention the arrival and development of the main, standard-gauge railways. That being the case, in following the routes of the various lines, I have included other features and railways of later date so as to assist as far as possible the identification of those parts of the former courses that have been completely obliterated.

Eric R. Shepherd
Plympton
Plymouth
March 1997

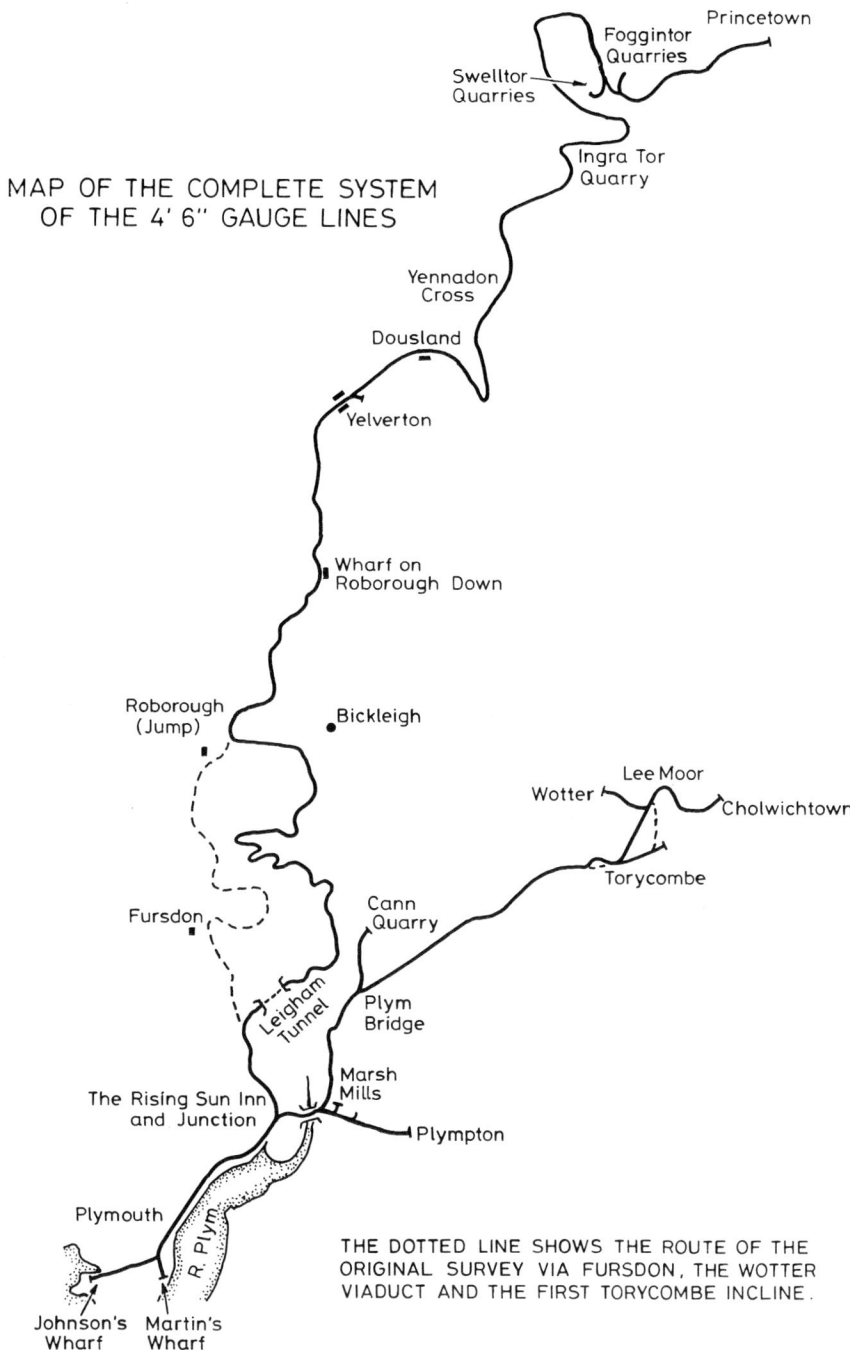

THE ROUTES DESCRIBED

As the longest and earliest of the railways, it is appropriate to commence by tracing the main route of the Plymouth & Dartmoor Railway, which, in its completed form, extended over a distance of 25½ miles. An interesting feature was the provision of milestones along its course; these were cut from granite and each resembled a stone-roller set on its end, the top of which was cut at an angle and incised with a 'mileage' number.

The course of the line can conveniently be divided into four sections – from Sutton Harbour, Plymouth to Leigham Tunnel, from Leigham Tunnel to Roborough, from Roborough to Yennadon Cross and from Yennadon Cross to the Quarries and Princetown:–

1. Sutton Harbour, Plymouth to Leigham Tunnel.

The southern terminus was situated at a quay (or wharf) on the eastern side of Sutton Harbour in the Port of Plymouth, known as Coxside. This quay also came to be known as Johnson's Quay, a name that would figure prominently in the history of the undertaking.

From the terminus, the line initially ran in an easterly direction, presently crossing the road leading to the Laira Iron Bridge and forming a triangular junction with the branch to Laira (or Martin's) Wharf that passed under the same road a short distance to the south. At this point, the branch shared a bridge with the London & South Western Railway's line to the Cattewater before crossing this later line on the level and proceeding to its terminus, which was situated alongside the estuary of the River Plym, immediately to the south of Iron Bridge. Here, on the western side of the bridge, a siding served a nearby granite works.

A modern-day photograph of the bridge shared by the L & SWR's line to the Cattewater and the Plymouth & Dartmoor Railway's branch to Martin's Wharf, which came in from the right of the picture.

The Plymouth & Dartmoor Railway and the Lee Moor Tramway in the Plymouth area, and their routes in relation to the later, standard-gauge railways

Details of the 4ft. 6in. gauge lines

1. Sutton Harbour
2. Johnson's Wharf
3. Level-crossing of 4ft. 6in. and 4ft. 8½in. gauge lines
4. Martin's Wharf
5. Original terminus of the P.&D.R.
6. The Rising Sun Inn and junction
7. Leigham Tunnel
8. P.&D.R. route to Princetown
9. Bridge over River Plym and Weighbridge Cottage
10. Branch to end of Cann Quarry canal at Marsh Mills
11. Route to Cann Quarry
12. Branch to Farm Quarry
13. Terminus of Plympton Branch
14. Junction of Cann Quarry line and Lee Moor Tramway
15. Route to Lee Moor and Cann Wood incline

Details of the 4ft. 8½in. gauge lines

16. Plympton Station and route to Exeter
17. Tavistock Junction
18. Marsh Mills Station
19. Siding to clay works at Marsh Mills
20. Siding to War Department depot at Coypool
21. Plym Bridge Halt
22. Route to Tavistock and Launceston
23. Laira Junction
24. Laira Depot and sidings
25. Lipson Junction
26. Mount Gould Junction
27. Mutley Tunnel and route to Plymouth and Cornwall
28. Cattewater Junction
29. Friary Station
30. Cattewater branch
31. Plymstock Station
32. Route to Turnchapel
33. Route to Yealmpton
34. Estuary of the River Plym

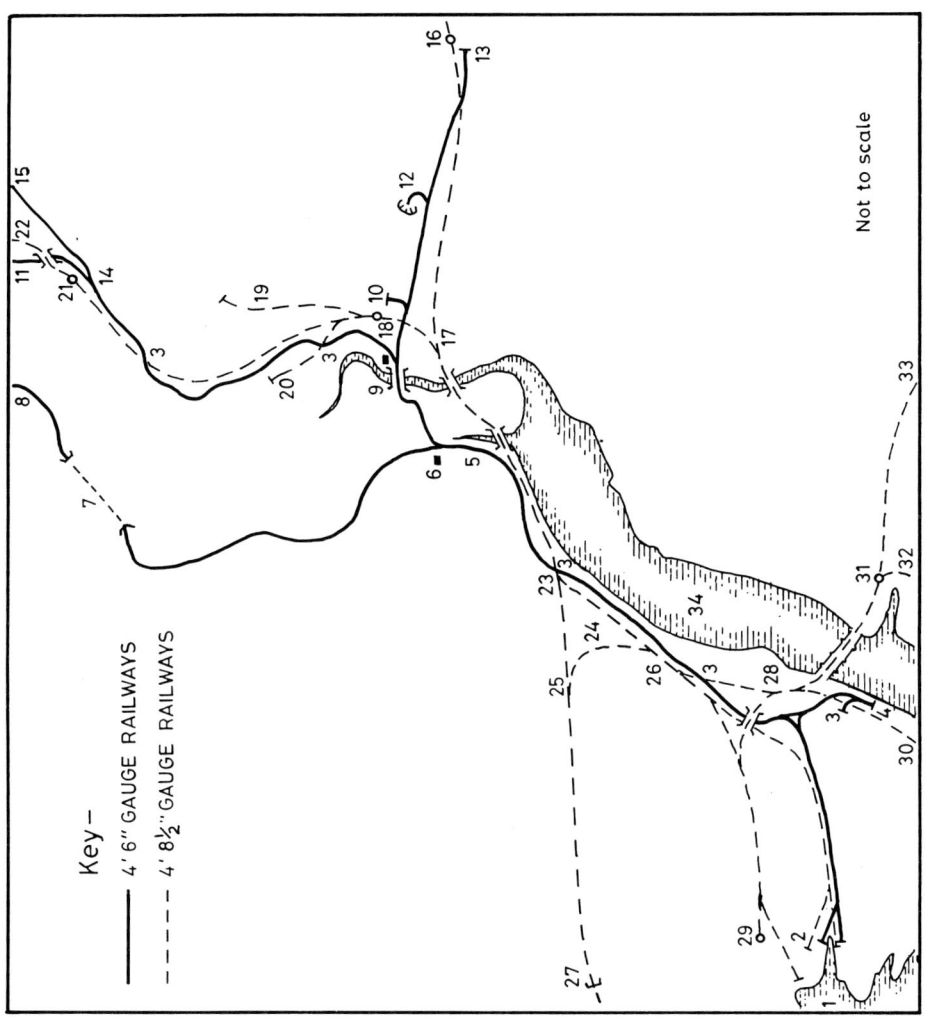

The main line that we are following, however, passed under Embankment Road by means of a bridge soon after leaving the junction just mentioned. It then went under another bridge, which carried the L & SWR line to the Cattewater, and emerged in close proximity to a concrete works that was of great significance in the years leading up to the closure of the last part of the system. Beyond the concrete works, it was not long before a second crossing of a standard-gauge railway on the level occurred, on this occasion being that of the Great Western Railway's line to Yealmpton. Thereafter, the line proceeded to pass Mount Gould Junction and curved to run between the sidings of the GWR Laira Engine Sheds on the left and Embankment Road on the right, where transfer sidings with the GWR were once provided.

The line shown crossing the GWR Yealmpton branch prior to reaching Mount Gould Junction.

At the end of the sidings, the railway shared a level-crossing with the main GWR line from Paddington, the crossing being controlled from Laira Signal

A view of Laira Crossing from Embankment Road, with the boarded walkway between the rails clearly visible. The signal guarding the crossing is the second from the right.

The stretch of line running past the site of the original terminus, which was situated behind the bushes to the left of the picture. In the background can be seen the short siding that was provided on the eastern side as the line approached the main road from Plympton to Plymouth, near Crabtree.

The line shown crossing the main road from Plympton to Plymouth, near Crabtree. By the time that this photograph was taken in the mid-1950s, however, the junction on the far side of the road and the line to Princetown (which would have continued behind the parked car) had long since been removed.

Part of the southern section of the railway, probably near milepost 3 in the Forder Valley.

Courtesy of *The Railway Magazine*

Box and the space between the 4 ft. 6 in. gauge track being boarded so as to assist the horses as they hauled their trains over the standard-gauge lines. After passing through a gate on the northern side of the GWR, the line then turned north-eastwards. Upon doing so, it threaded a bridge under the northern end of Embankment Road, ran beside a small tidal lake bounded by the GWR line and continued past the hamlet of Lower Crabtree before curving northwards along the side of a narrow tidal creek – the site of the original terminus of the Plymouth & Dartmoor Railway. A little distance farther on, a short siding was provided on the eastern side as the line approached the main road from Plympton to Plymouth, which was crossed on the level; the crossing was ungated and was situated just to the east of the Rising Sun Inn at Crabtree.

On the far side of the road, there was a junction: the line to Princetown continued straight ahead past Marsh House, whilst the other line – to Marsh Mills, Cann Quarry, Plympton and Lee Moor – rounded a sharp curve and took up a position behind a low stone wall at the side of the road. The original line, meanwhile, continued across a wide valley and then, from an elevation of only 18 feet above sea-level, entered the first stage of its long climb to Dartmoor by rising on a substantial embankment that carried it to the hillside on the northern side of the valley. From here, it curved through a cutting and intersected, by means of a level-crossing, the road leading up the Forder Valley. Then, following the contours around the hillside, the line climbed gradually away from the road, turned north-eastwards and entered a small side valley before reaching the southern end of Leigham Tunnel, where there was another short siding.

The tunnel, one of the earliest railway tunnels in the country, was faced with dressed stone at both portals and was 620 yards in length. The bore was quite straight, but not large, having a height of 9 feet 6 inches and a width of 8 feet 6 inches. It was unlined for most of its length and, although comparatively small, was adequate for the purpose that it served.

The southern portal of Leigham Tunnel, as photographed in the mid-1950s with corrugated iron doors.

2. Leigham Tunnel to Roborough (Jump).

The northern portal of Leigham Tunnel, with the standing figure indicating the smallness of the bore.

On emerging from the northern portal of the tunnel, opposite some dwellings named Tunnel Cottages, the line ran along the side of a minor road leading to Plym Bridge. This, however, was over only a short distance as before long it was taking up a position on the western side of the valley of the River Plym. Gaining height as it followed the wooded hillside, the line then went on to reach a deep, curving cutting before running over a substantial embankment on a sharp bend; the first of several such earthworks that carried the line over streams running down the small side valleys in the woods.

The road from Plym Bridge to Roborough was crossed by an underline bridge, and the valley side steepened considerably as the forbidding workings of Rumple Quarry, served by a siding, appeared on both sides of the line. Immediately below at this point, on the eastern side of the valley, was the extensive excavation of Cann Slate Quarry, also served by a branch of the railway.

Continuing its curving course, the railway crossed another side valley prior to passing lineside cottages near Riverford. It then entered an even more tortuous section: seen on a map, the line here resembled the outstretched thumb and three fingers of a hand as it crossed no less than four more side valleys in Holt Wood before emerging and rounding a curve to cross an embankment by Darklake Farm, at a height of almost 400 feet above sea-level.

Now running through fields, the railway was able to pursue a much straighter course as it passed within sight of Bickleigh Village and headed away from the Plym Valley. Eventually, it had to cross Blackeven Hill and another minor road on the level, before reaching the eastern side of the main road from Plymouth to Tavistock, just to the north of the village of Roborough, or Jump, as it was formerly named.

The line approaching Darklake Farm, with milepost 8 just visible where the track disappears behind bushes.
Courtesy of *The Railway Magazine*

3. Roborough (Jump) to Yennadon Cross.

The road to Bickleigh was crossed on the level (as were almost all the roads which confronted the course of the railway) and, after running at the side of the road to Tavistock for a short distance, the line turned away to pass through fields behind Higher Leigh Farm. It then went across Little Down Lane prior to curving to the north and reaching the open common land which formed the southern part of Roborough Down.

A siding was sited here on the eastern side, and the railway then followed a curving route across the Down, presently crossing the Plymouth Leat, Roborough Down Lane, and the road to Clearbrook. After that, the line passed through a shallow cutting, beyond which, on the eastern side, was an isolated building – sited at what was almost exactly the half-way point of the railway. This, in fact, had been constructed as a depot (or wharf) for the

The wharf/stable depot sited between mileposts 11 & 12.

15

railway, but had also been used for stabling the horses that were employed to haul the trains. Close at hand, there was also a siding that had been laid with granite rather than iron rails, one side of the stone being dressed to a straight edge so as to accommodate the flanges of the wheels of the wagons.

As the line proceeded towards Yelverton it was joined, on the western side, by the Devonport Leat and, on the eastern side, by the Plymouth Leat, and ran between fields for a short distance. It then took up a position on the edge of Roborough Down until eventually crossing both the Devonport Leat and the road to Princetown to arrive at Yelverton. Here, the line ran across the green between The Tors and the Rock Hotel (near which was a walled wharf compound approached by a curving siding laid with more granite rails) and had, by now, attained a height of 625 feet above sea-level.

Beyond Yelverton, the line passed through more fields and, after crossing a minor road leading to Lake, presently came alongside the Princetown road as it headed north-eastwards towards Dousland. Shortly afterwards, the line also crossed the road leading to Meavy and then turned southwards at the commencement of a remarkable length of railway where the line doubled back on itself in order to gain height: this was achieved by allowing the line to continue running in a southerly direction, passing through fields on either side of Iron Mine Lane and on to open moorland at the southern edge of Yennadon, and then directing it over a low embankment built roughly in the form of a horse-shoe. Consequently, the line now ran in a northerly direction along the western edge of the Down, after which it passed through enclosures and across the Princetown road (again) at Yennadon Cross, situated near the foot of Peek Hill and at a height of 825 feet above sea-level.

4. Yennadon Cross to the Quarries and Princetown.

Having crossed the road, the line continued in a northerly direction, running through fields and being carried over the lane to Peekhill Farm by an underline bridge, one of very few on the railway. Onwards past Horseyeatt

A modern-day photograph looking towards Princetown from near Yennadon Cross. The earthworks of the former bridge over the lane to Peekhill Farm are in the field nearest to the camera, beyond which the curving wall denotes where the line headed through further fields before reaching the open moor of Walkhampton Common.

Farm, the route lay through more enclosures and then, at a height of 900 feet above sea-level, the open moor of Walkhampton Common was reached. Thereafter, apart from passing through a small area of enclosed land to the east of Routrundle Farm, the railway continued on open moorland, following the contours of the hillsides so as to gain height and presently attaining 1,000 feet at Ingra Tor. Here, a sharp curve around the tor changed the railway's direction from north-west to east and took it past Ingra Tor Quarry – a deep excavation approached through a narrow cutting on the southern side of the line.

Continuing towards Princetown, a shallow cutting took the railway to the foot of another remarkable section of the line – the great loop around King's Tor, which enabled it to climb from 1,075 to 1,250 feet above sea-level. The railway first followed a curve, which took it in a semi-circular route to cross the Yes Tor Brook by means of a masonry bridge, and then ran north-westwards, climbing along the side of the hill on which stand Swell Tor and

The downstream portal of the bridge over the Yes Tor Brook.

King's Tor. As the line turned to the east on a sharp curve above Hucken Tor, a magnificent view, possibly the finest on the whole railway, unfolded across the Walkham Valley and the countryside to the west. Beyond this, the line ran to the south-east on its way to a point a mere one quarter of a mile from its course at the commencement of the loop, but having, in the meantime, covered a distance of 2 miles! Within this loop were situated several of the granite quarries which provided the railway with its principal source of traffic, and which were served by an inclined plane and sidings; further sidings served more quarries at Foggintor, on the eastern side of the line.

The final stage of the railway ran eastwards along the lower slopes of North Hessary Tor, presently passing through the site of the later GWR Princetown Station and its approach road. It then entered the village, where it ran across the Square to terminate at a depot named The Railway Inn, having attained a height of almost 1,375 feet above sea-level.

The journey from Plymouth must have been a long and arduous one, both for the waggoners and the horses, particularly in adverse weather, but the building of the line was a remarkable achievement in those early days of 'the Railway Age'.

Having followed the principal route of the railway, it is now necessary to examine the routes of the other lines which diverged near the Rising Sun Inn at Crabtree:–

The railway to Marsh Mills.

The junction with the junction with the line to Princetown line was situated immediately to the north of the level-crossing over the main road at Crabtree. Then, as previously stated, the line to Marsh Mills (and also to Cann Quarry, Plympton and Lee Moor) rounded a sharp curve and took up a position behind a low stone wall at the side of the road. This, in fact, resulted in the line running in a north-easterly direction.

After reaching Longbridge, the line continued, for a short distance, to run at the western side of the Forder Valley road until crossing it on the level by means of a very sharp curve and passing over the River Plym on a two-span iron-girder bridge. A dwelling known as Weighbridge Cottage stood on the northern side of the line on the eastern bank of the river; here the line to Marsh Mills continued straight ahead and, after a short distance, terminated at the basin of the canal which had come down the Plym Valley from the Cann Quarry.

The railway to Cann Quarry.

This line branched from the route to Marsh Mills at Weighbridge Cottage and, after passing a siding, ran by the river-side to within a short distance of the GWR line to Tavistock near Marsh Mills Station, there turning north up the Plym Valley to run on the western side of the later railway.

The GWR branch presently passed into a deep cutting and here the Cann Quarry line ran alongside the Cann Quarry Canal, curving away from, and then returning to, the other railway with the river some way below it on the western side. This was followed, after a short distance, by the two railways crossing one another diagonally on the level, which, in turn, meant that the Cann Quarry line was now situated between the GWR, on its western side, and the canal, on its eastern side.

The level-crossing between Marsh Mills and Plym Bridge.

Approaching Plym Bridge, the Lee Moor Tramway diverged on the eastern side, crossing the canal on its way to the foot of the Cann Wood incline. The Cann Quarry line, however, continued to run beside the canal until reaching the point where the Lee Moor Tramway recrossed the waterway and began the ascent of the incline. The line then left the canal and ran alongside the retaining wall of the incline before reaching and crossing the road from Plympton to Plym Bridge on the level: the GWR route passed over this road by a bridge immediately on the western side, whilst the Cann Quarry line ran under the GWR through a bridge which it shared with the canal. Thereafter, the two railways ran side by side, with the GWR climbing away on the eastern side, until the canal entered a tunnel and the Cann Quarry line traversed a sharp curve directly above the river. The line then ran under the GWR Cann Viaduct to arrive at its terminus in the quarry.

(At the time of the Cann Quarry line's construction the GWR (originally the South Devon & Tavistock Railway) had not, of course, arrived on the scene, but the two railways ran in such close proximity that it is difficult to separate them when describing the route up the valley).

The railway to Plympton.

A further section of the system was an extension of the branch serving the canal basin at Marsh Mills; this was constructed along the northern side of the road leading to Plympton, and ran to a depot which adjoined St. Mary's Bridge, at the lower end of Plympton St. Mary. There was also a short branch which led off northwards about half a mile from Marsh Mills, passed through a short tunnel and reached Farm Quarry, situated near Great Woodford Farm.

The railway to Lee Moor.

The final part of the railways to be described, and the last to be built, is the Lee Moor Tramway. Diverging from the Cann Quarry Railway as it approached Plym Bridge, the tramway crossed the canal and reached the foot of the Cann Wood incline where sidings were provided, together with brick-built stables for the horses used on the trains to and from the southern end of the line. As the ascent of the incline was commenced, the canal was recrossed twice before the tramway passed over the Plym Bridge to Plympton road by means of a wooden trestle bridge, and entered the woods. The incline was $1^1/_4$ miles in length, and lifted the line 330 feet to the drum-house at the summit. It was operated by gravity, the loaded trains being mainly in the downward direction.

A passing loop was situated at the mid point of the incline, the upper section being laid with three rails so that the centre rail could be used by trains in both directions. Below the loop, the up and down lines had separate rails, but these were interlaced so as to enable the tracks to pass through a

Looking up the Cann Wood incline.
B. Y. Williams, courtesy of *The Railway Magazine*

THE LEE MOOR TRAMWAY — CANN WOOD INCLINE

NOTICE

CANN WOOD INCLINE

MAXIMUM LOAD ON THIS

INCLINE NOT TO EXCEED

14 TONS ON TWO AXLES

English Clays Lovering
Pochin & Co. Ltd.,
St. Austell

NOTICE

EMPLOYEES ARE FORBIDDEN

TO WALK OR WORK ON THIS

INCLINE WHEN ROPE IS IN

MOTION

English Clays Lovering
Pochin & Co. Ltd.,
St. Austell

THESE NOTICES WERE SITED ON THE INCLINE, A FEW YARDS UP FROM THE LOWER END.

narrow cutting. The steel haulage cables were supported on iron pulleys running in iron boxes set below the rails, or on rollers set in wooden supports. At the top of the incline, the tramway passed over a forestry track on an underline bridge and ran onto an embankment to the drum-house, which was situated below the rails. There were two winding drums, geared together so that the haulage cable on one was wound in as the other was paid out. A brake on the drums enabled the train speed to be controlled by a brake-lever, which was operated from above the level of the rails; the drum-house area had a roof over the tracks. Here, also, a siding and passing loop allowed marshalling of the trains, as this was the commencement of the locomotive-worked section of the tramway.

From the incline head, the tramway ran out of the woods and continued through fields to reach the Plympton to Shaugh Prior road at Whitegates level-crossing, which was gated and protected by signals; these were operated by the opening and shutting of the gates, the two being connected by a wire. A gateman's hut was also provided.

The Cann Wood incline commencing its descent through the woods: the change from four-rail to three-rail track can be seen a short distance in front of the camera.

The winding house at the summit of the Cann Wood incline, looking towards Torycombe.
    F.H.C. Casbourn, courtesy of The Stephenson Locomotive Society

The tramway between the summit of the Cann Wood incline and Whitegates level-crossing, looking towards Torycombe.

LEE MOOR TRAMWAY
Diagram of Whitegates Level Crossing

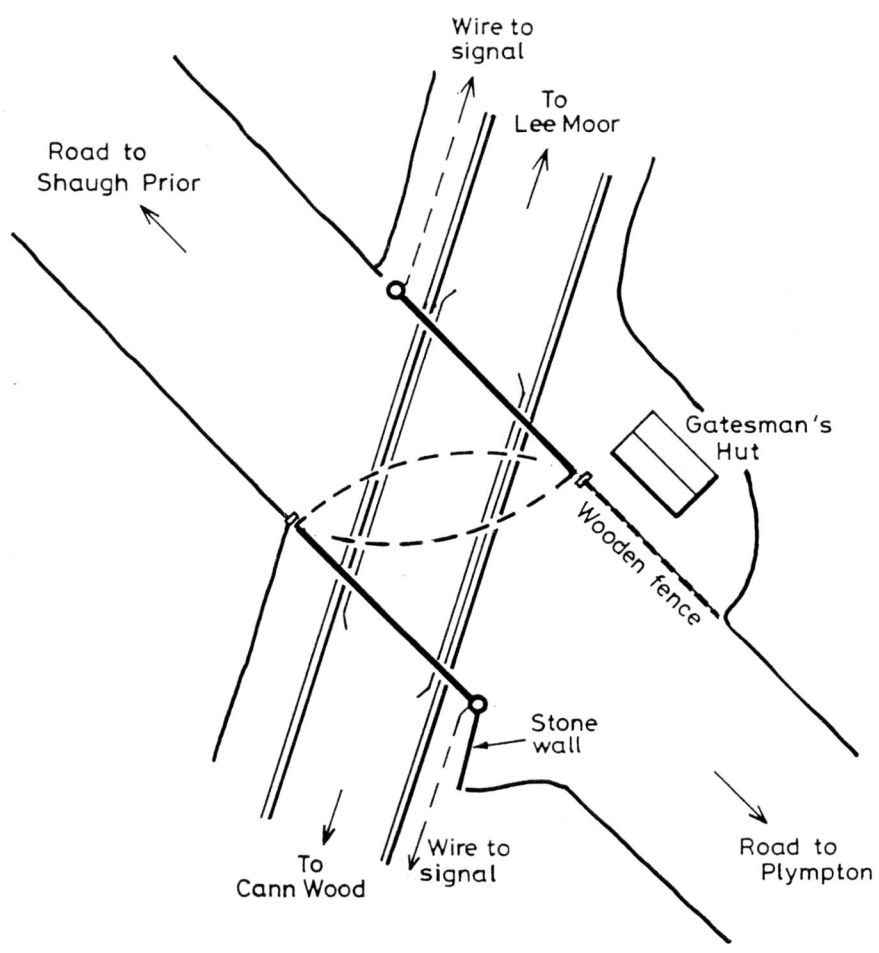

Whitegates level-crossing, with the gateman's hut beyond.

Continuing towards Lee Moor, the tramway ran under a minor road at Truelove Bridge and passed through a damp cutting and over an embankment leading past Coldstone Farm. There then followed a length of about half a mile along the hillside, at 400 feet above sea-level, before it crossed the valley of the Wotter Brook, initially by means of a timber viaduct; this, in turn, led the tramway to the area of the china clay works at Torycombe. Here, there were numerous sidings serving the various buildings and kilns, in addition to a brick and tile works farther up the valley. It was also here that the locomotive-worked part of the line terminated.

Loaded wagons standing out of use on the leaf-covered rails of the Wotter curve.

In the centre of the works area a level-crossing (ungated, but protected by signals) carried the Plympton to Lee Moor road across the tracks, whilst the locomotive shed was sited a short distance away on the western side of the crossing. One of the sidings on the northern side of the shed led to the Torycombe incline, which lifted the tramway to the village of Lee Moor, and which rose 300 feet in a distance of 700 yards. It was considerably steeper than the Cann Wood incline, and differed from it in that the portion below the passing loop was laid with a single line. Above the loop, the three-rail method was employed, as at Cann Wood. The drum-house was set back some distance from the top of the incline, the winding drum being below ground level; here, there was a single drum divided into two sections with one haulage cable taken from the top of the drum, and the other from the lower side, thus allowing one cable to be wound in as the other was paid out. The portion of the tramway above the drum-house was roofed over, as at Cann Wood.

Between the summit of the incline and the winding-house, a line led back around a sharp curve, passing a short siding serving a stone quarry and following the hillside to reach a further china clay works at Wotter.

A view from the Wotter branch approaching the summit of the Torycombe incline, which descends to the right of the picture. The stone block sleepers are plainly visible, as is the 'observation tower' facing down the incline.

Lens of Sutton

Returning to the drum-house, the tramway continued in a north-westerly direction, running on an embankment with a stone wall on the western side of the route and several terraces of houses on its eastern side. Reaching more open ground, further houses were passed on the western side, whilst a building used as a stable for the horses (set at a lower level) lay below on the opposite side of the line. Rounding a bend, the tramway crossed the road in the centre of Lee Moor village by an ungated level-crossing, immediately beyond which a siding ran towards the clay works' carpenters shop. It then curved to the south-east and continued on a level course, passing the works' power station and a winding engine-house for one of the waste tips, both of which were served by a siding. Beyond this, the tramway turned first to the east, and then to the north, crossing the Tory Brook on a high embankment, and the Cornwood to Lee Moor road by yet another ungated level-crossing, finally to terminate at the Cholwichtown clay works at an elevation of 740 feet above sea-level.

The Plymouth & Dartmoor Railway

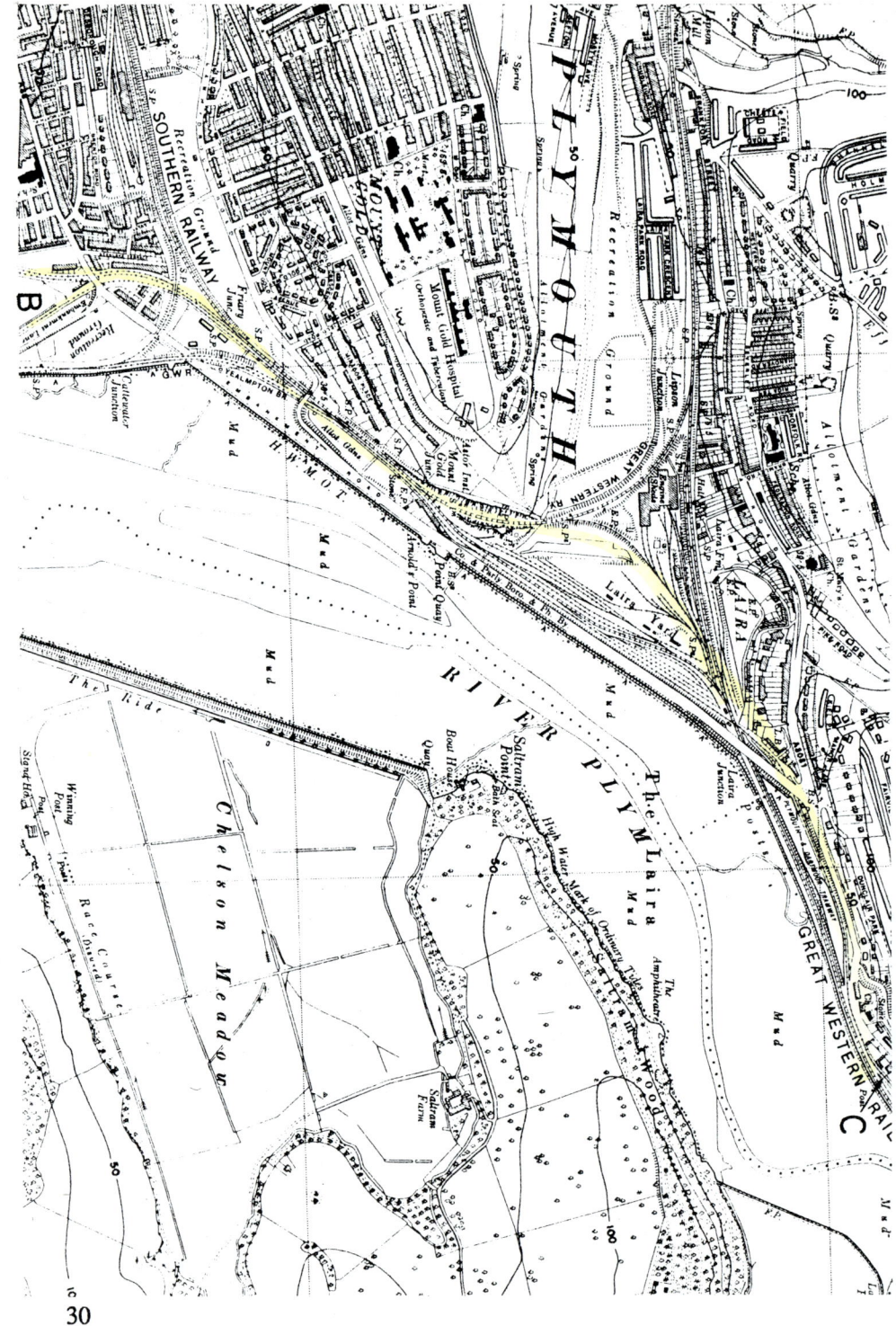

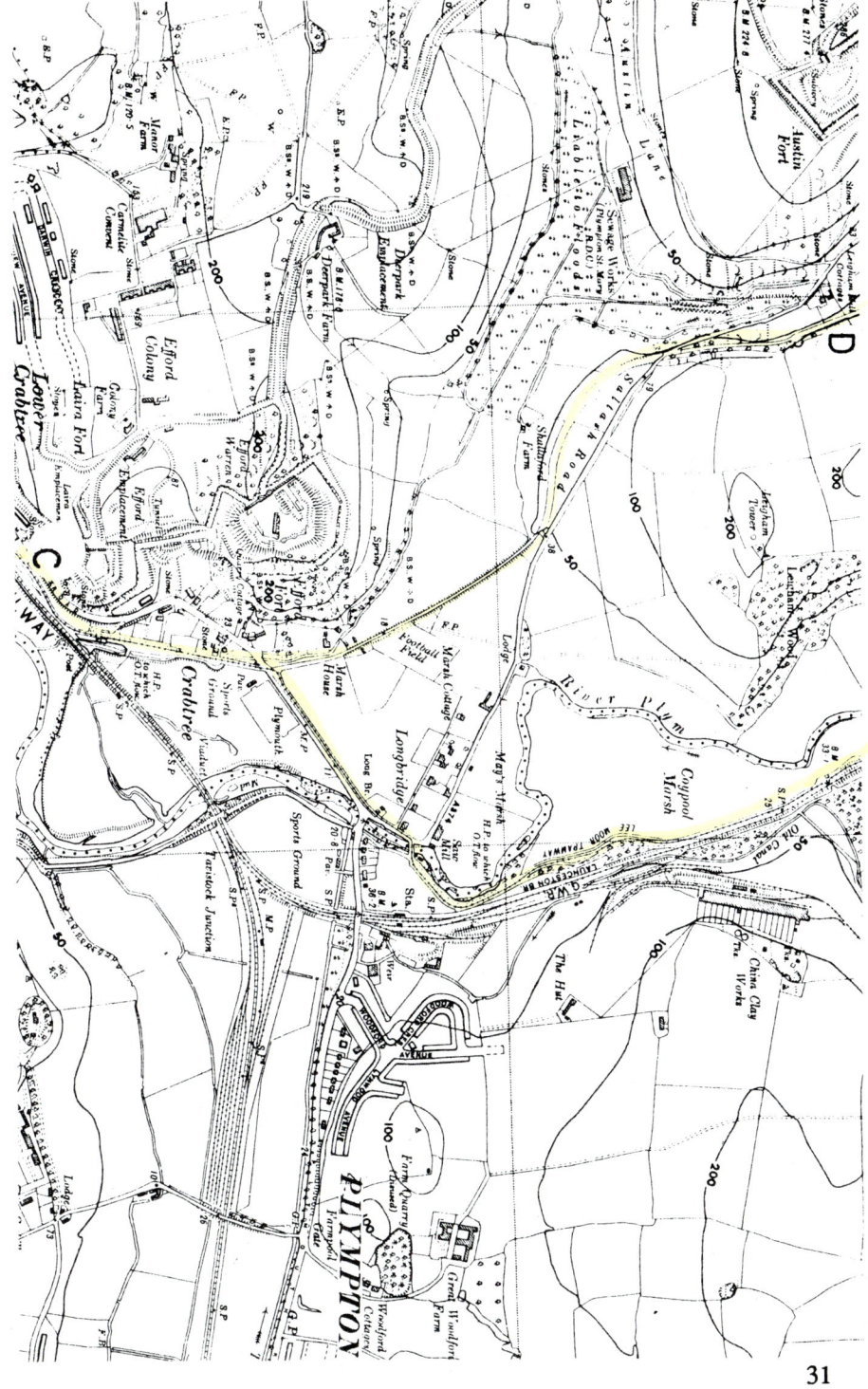

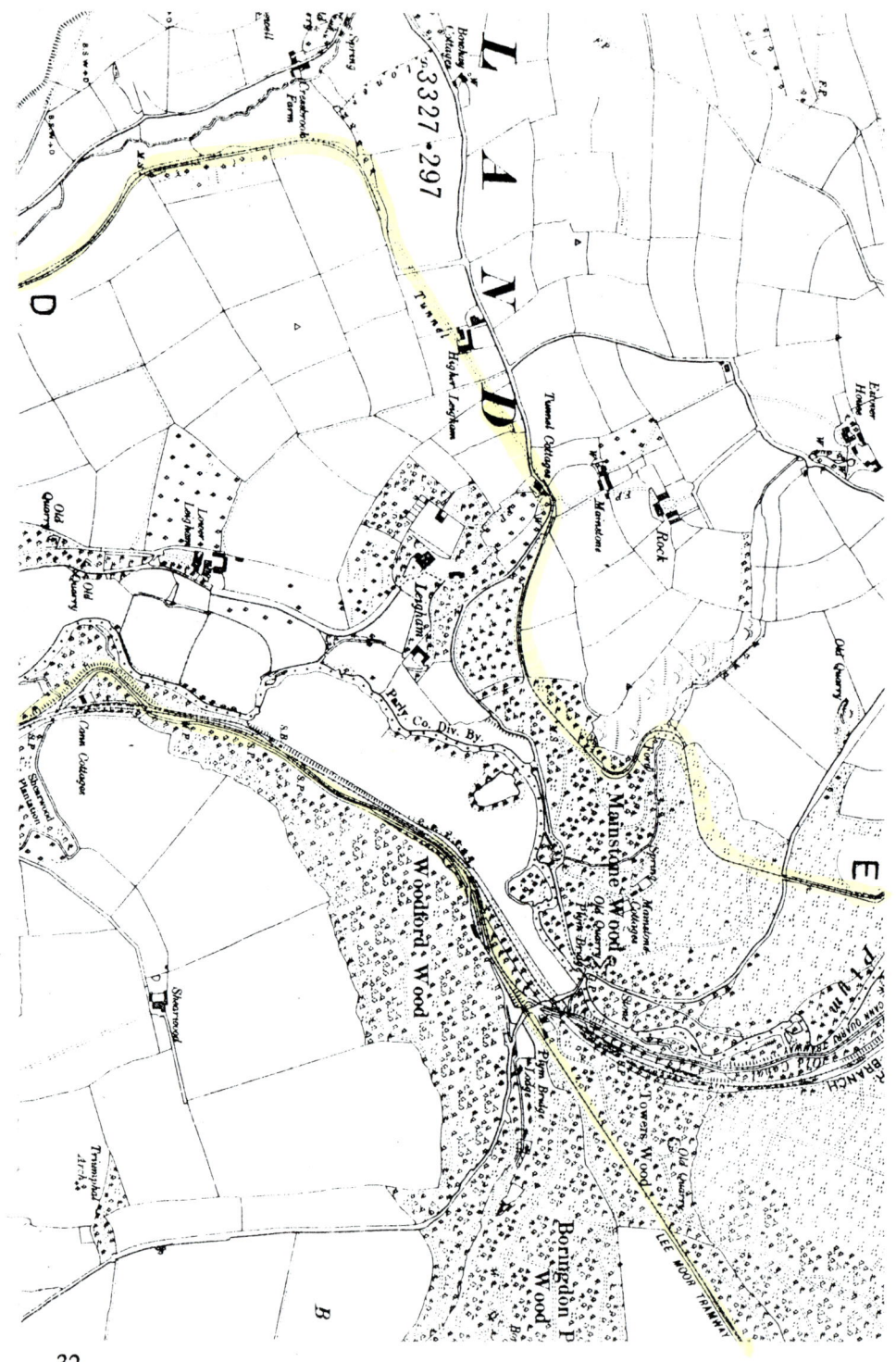

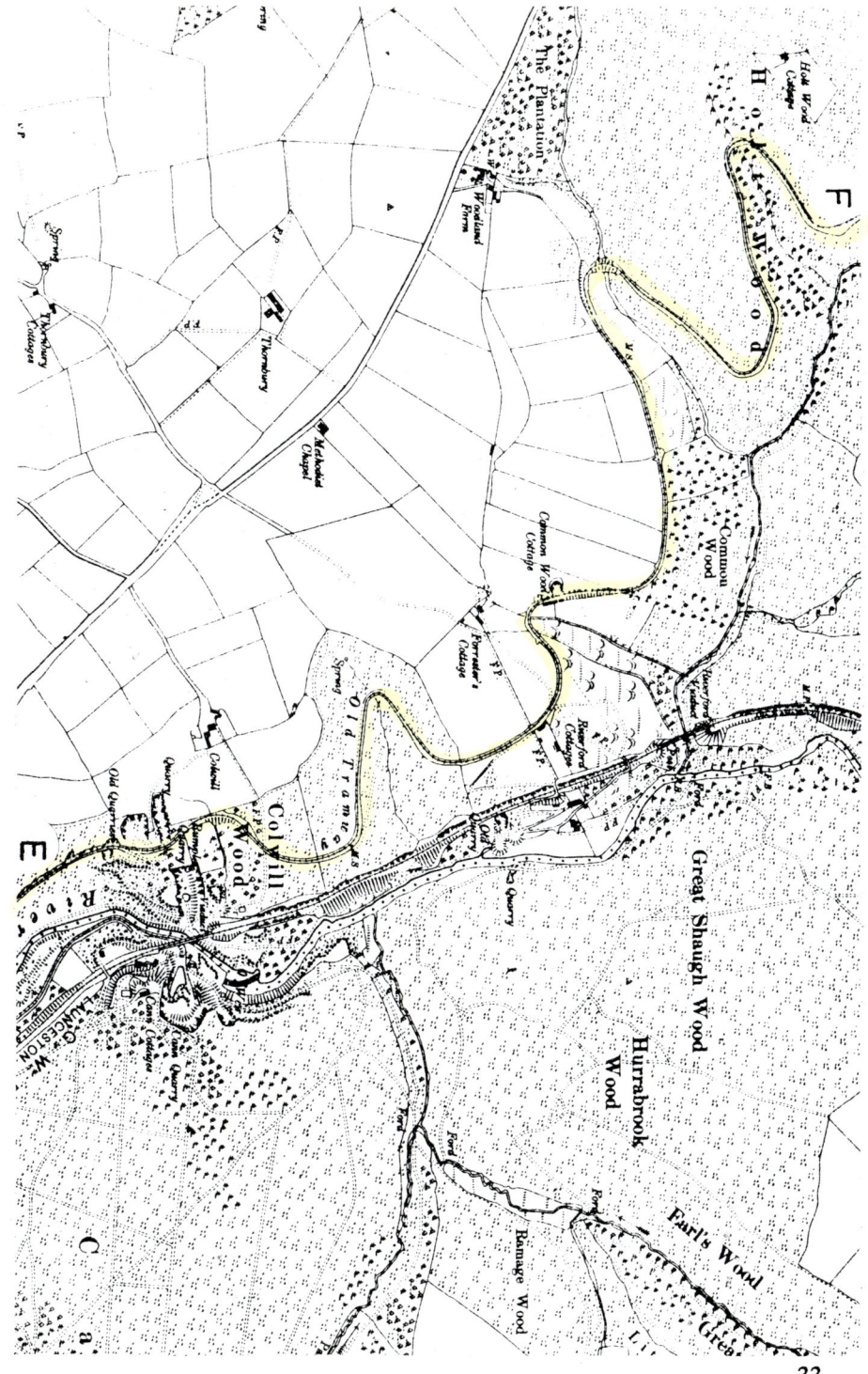

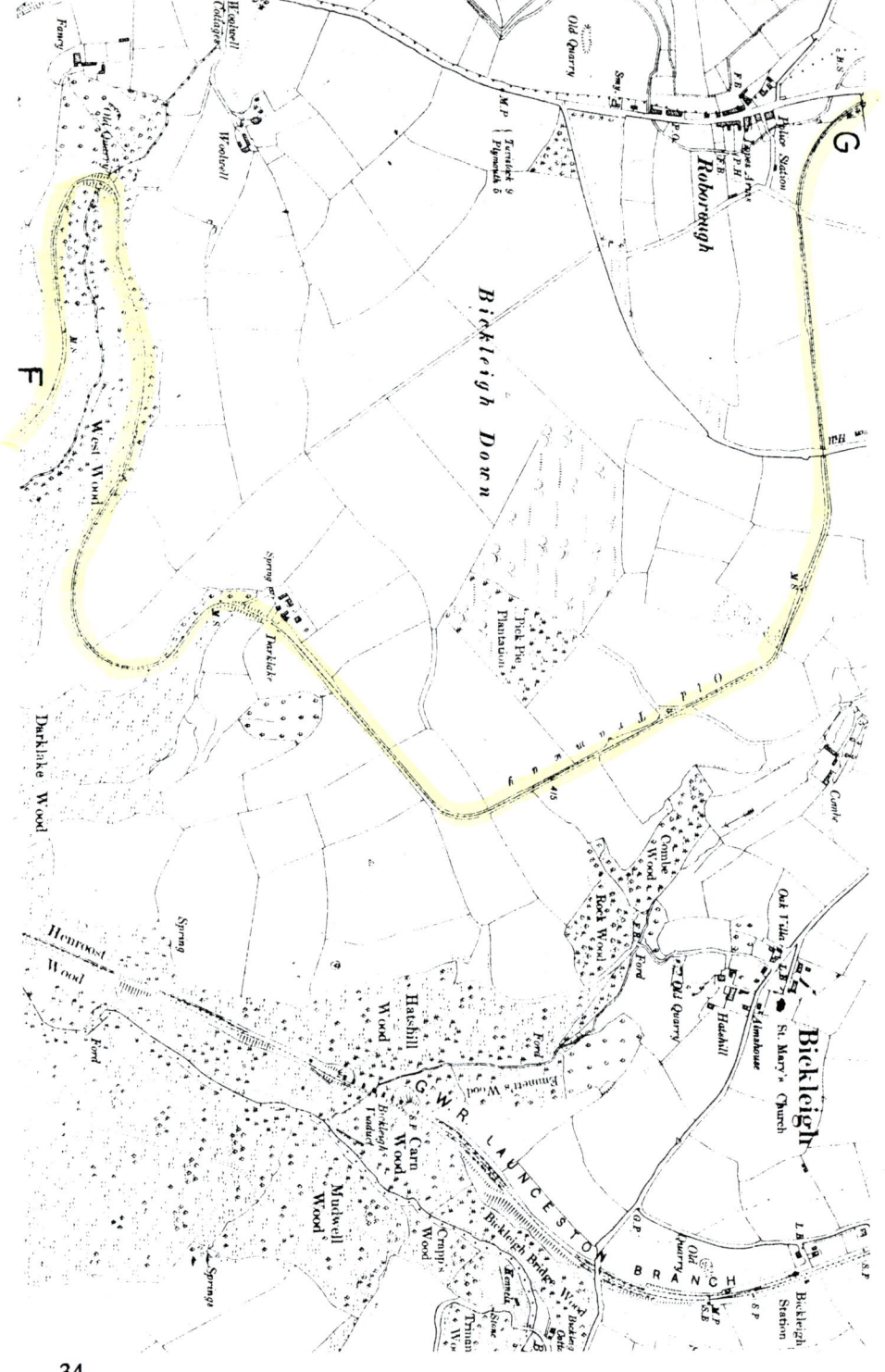

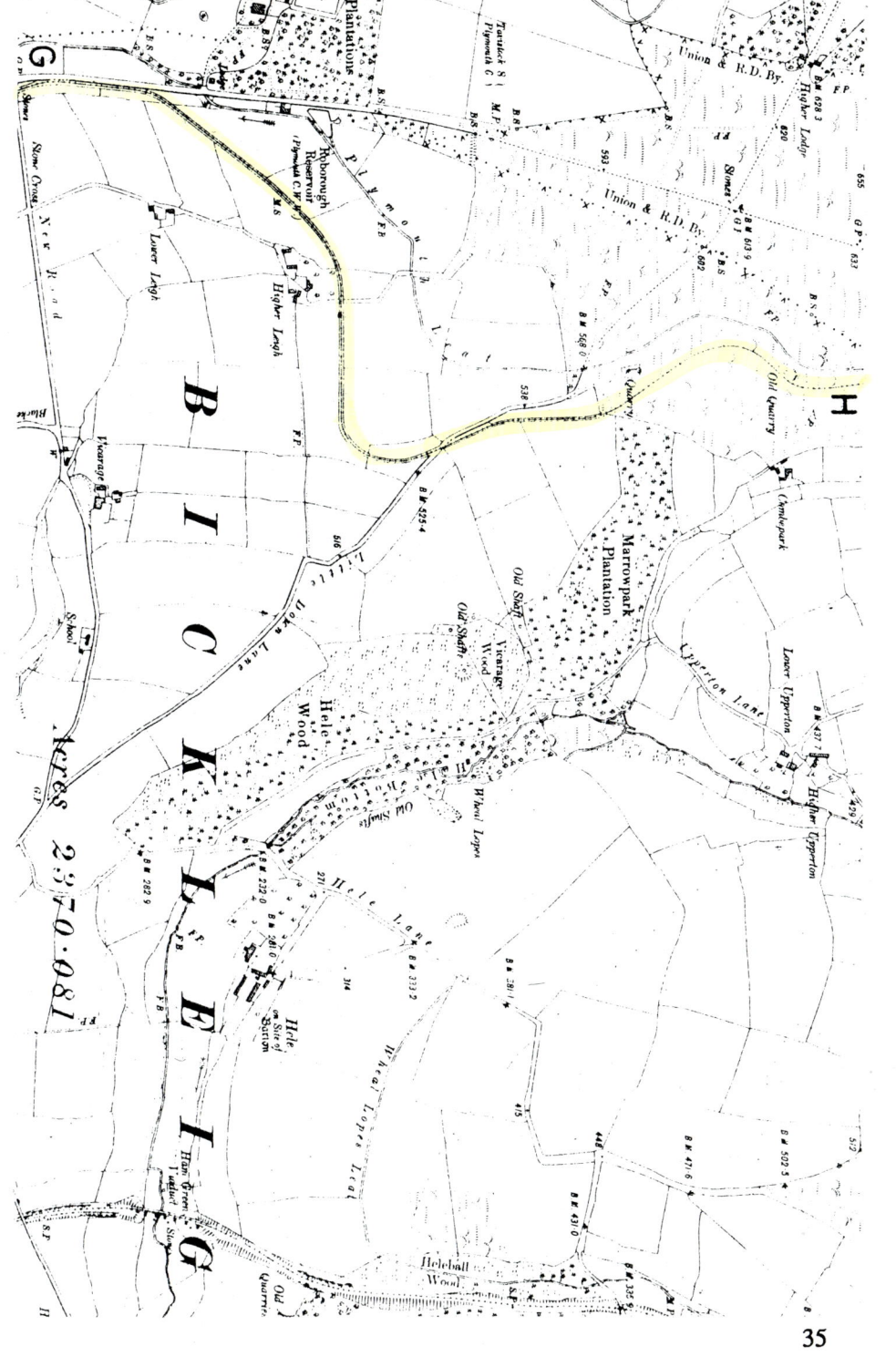

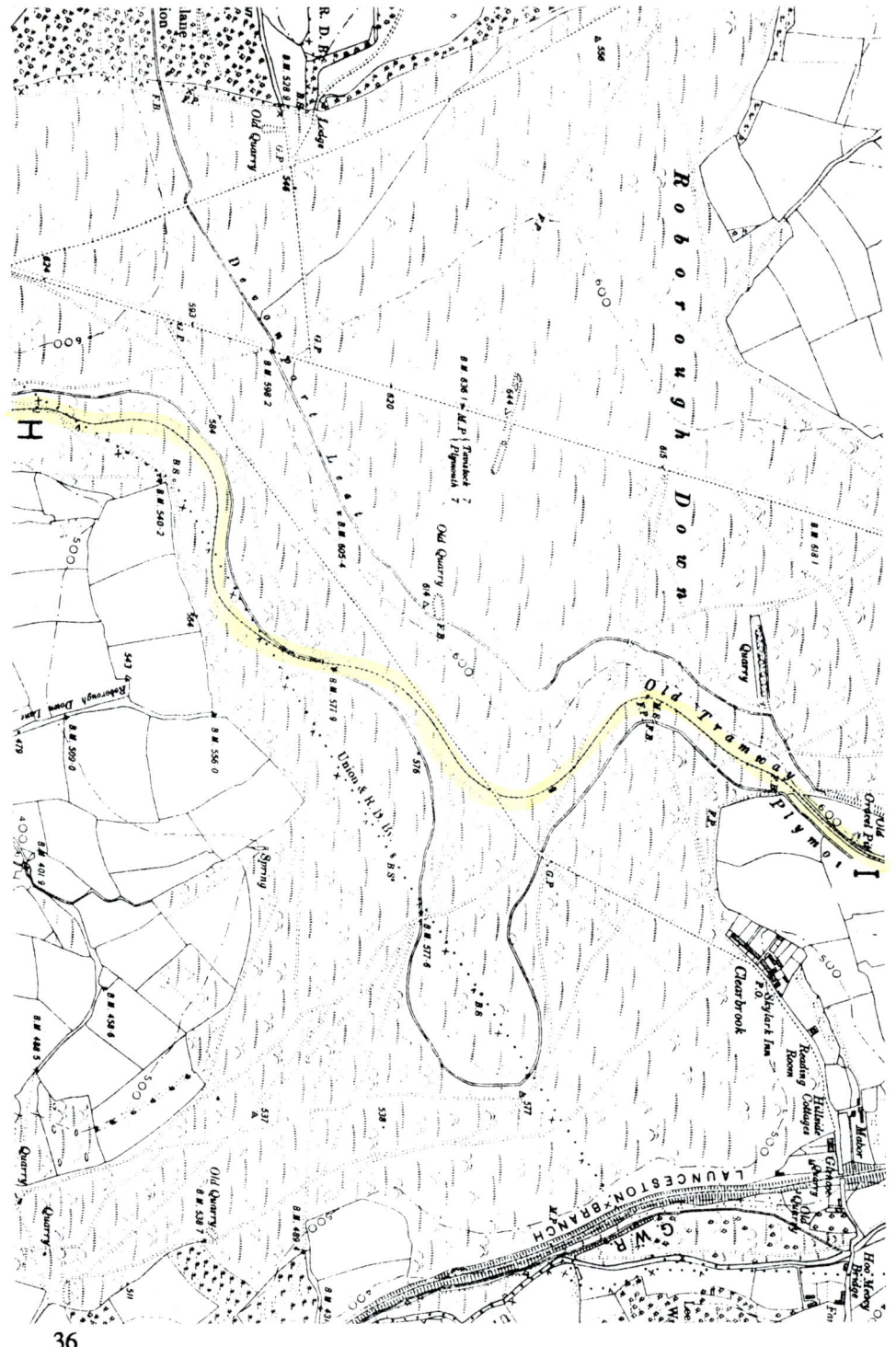

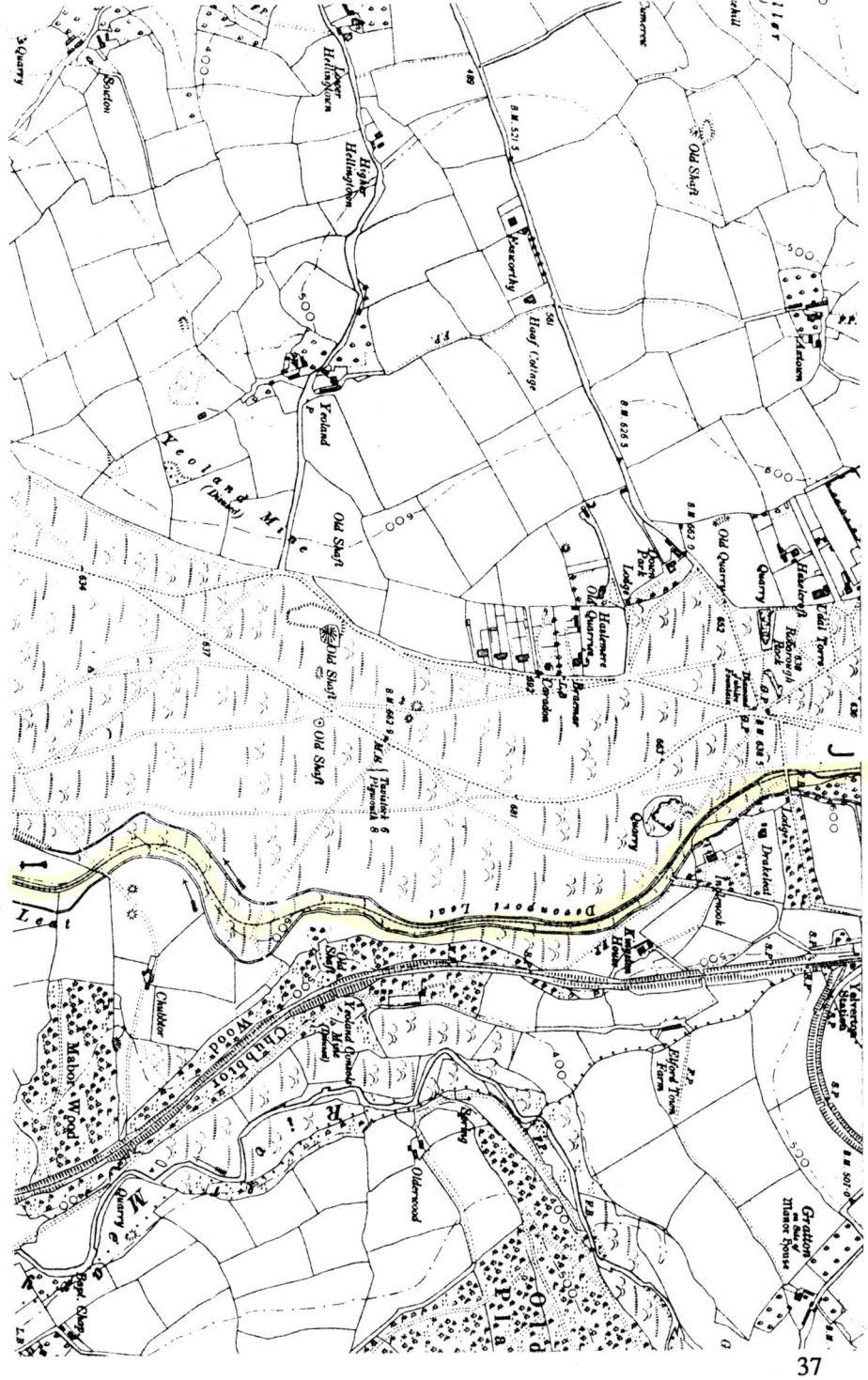

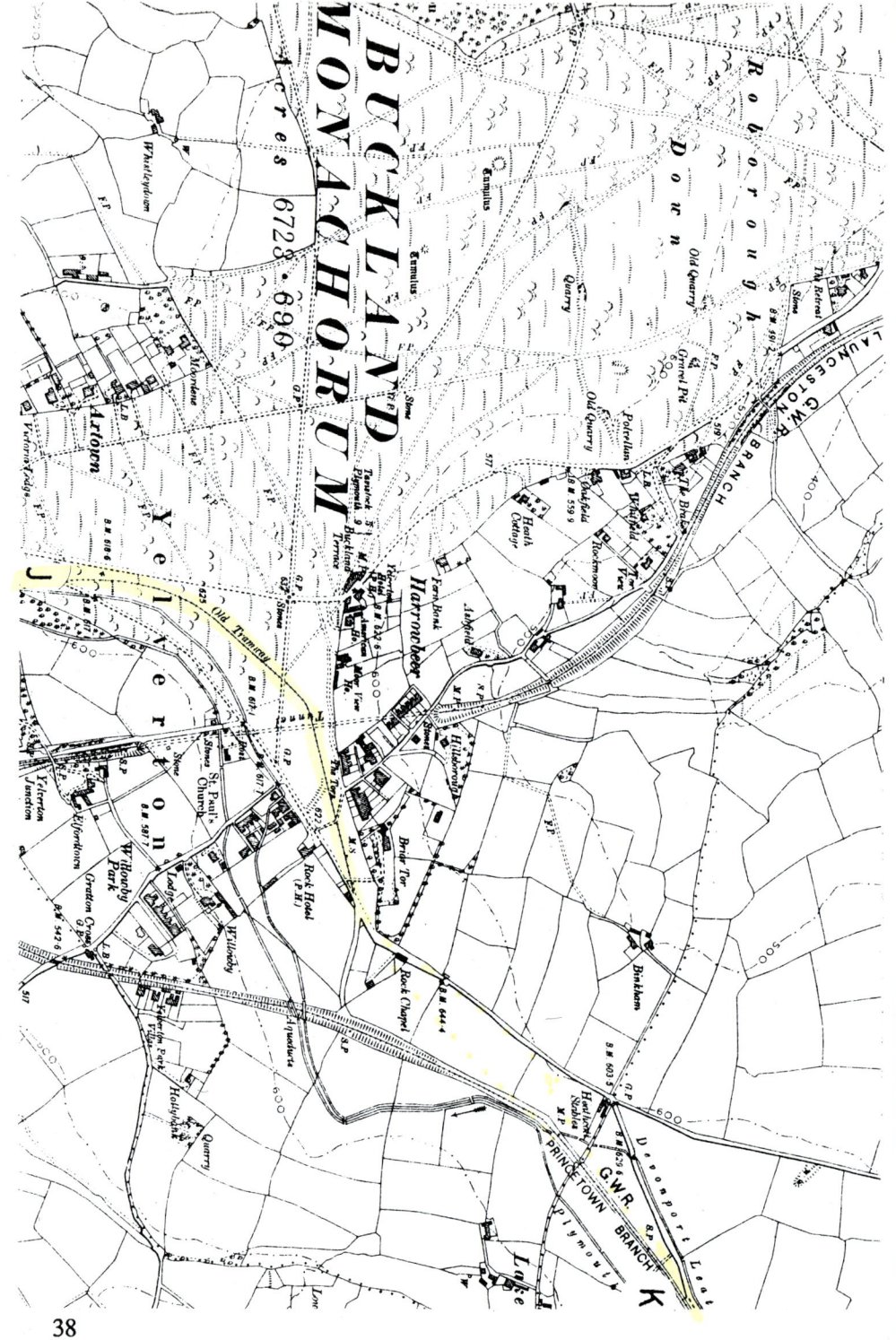

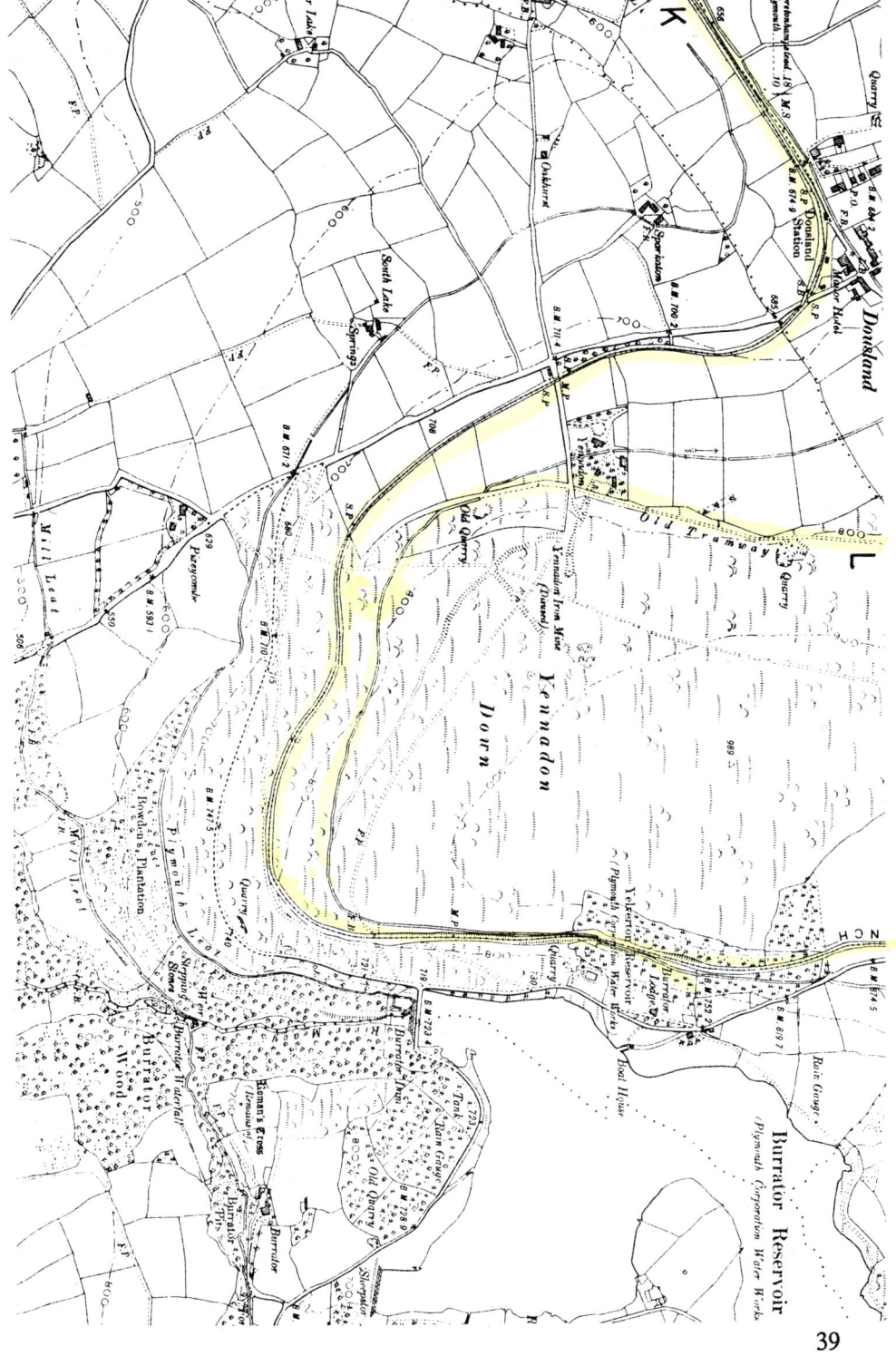

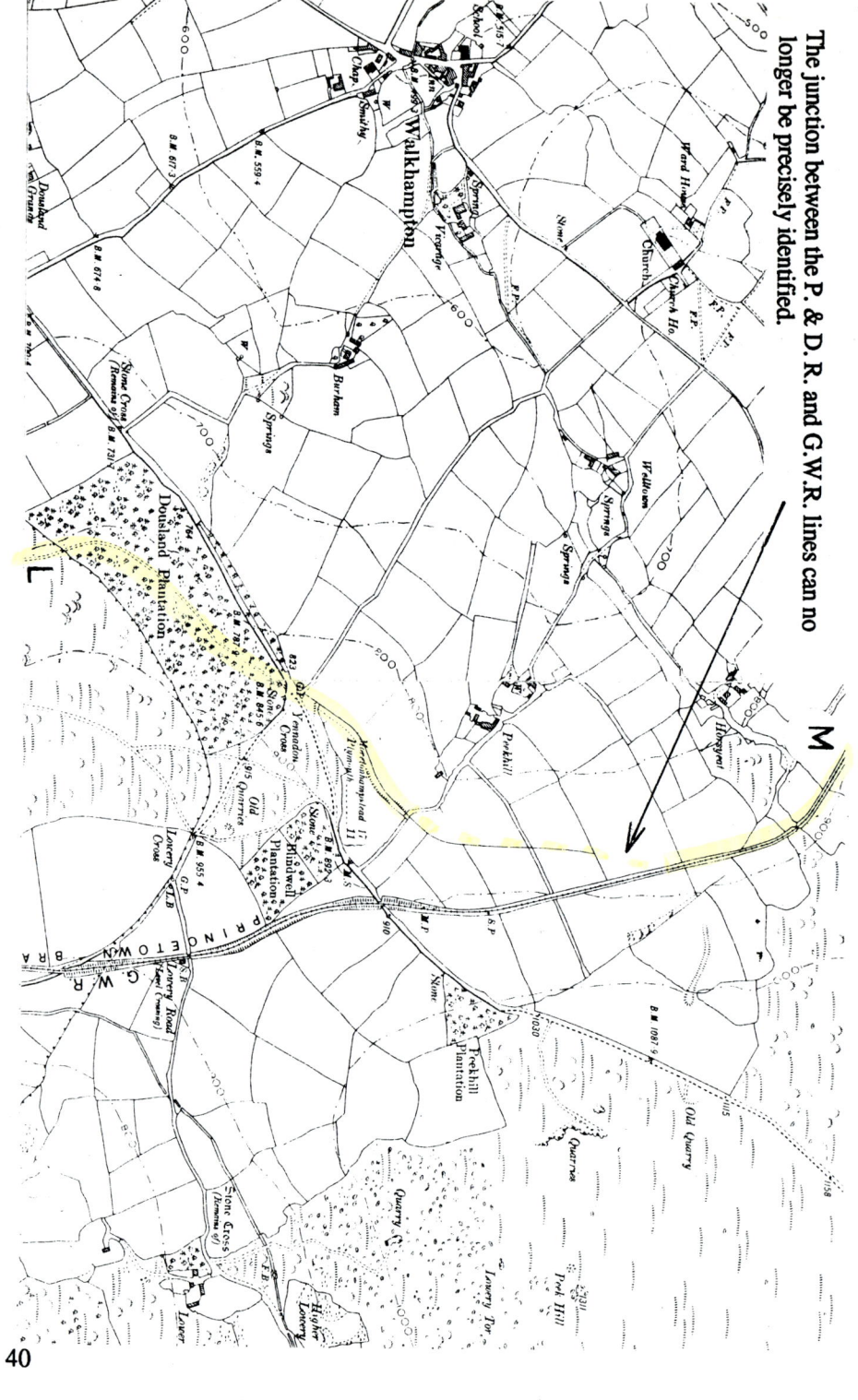

The junction between the P. & D. R. and G.W.R. lines can no longer be precisely identified.

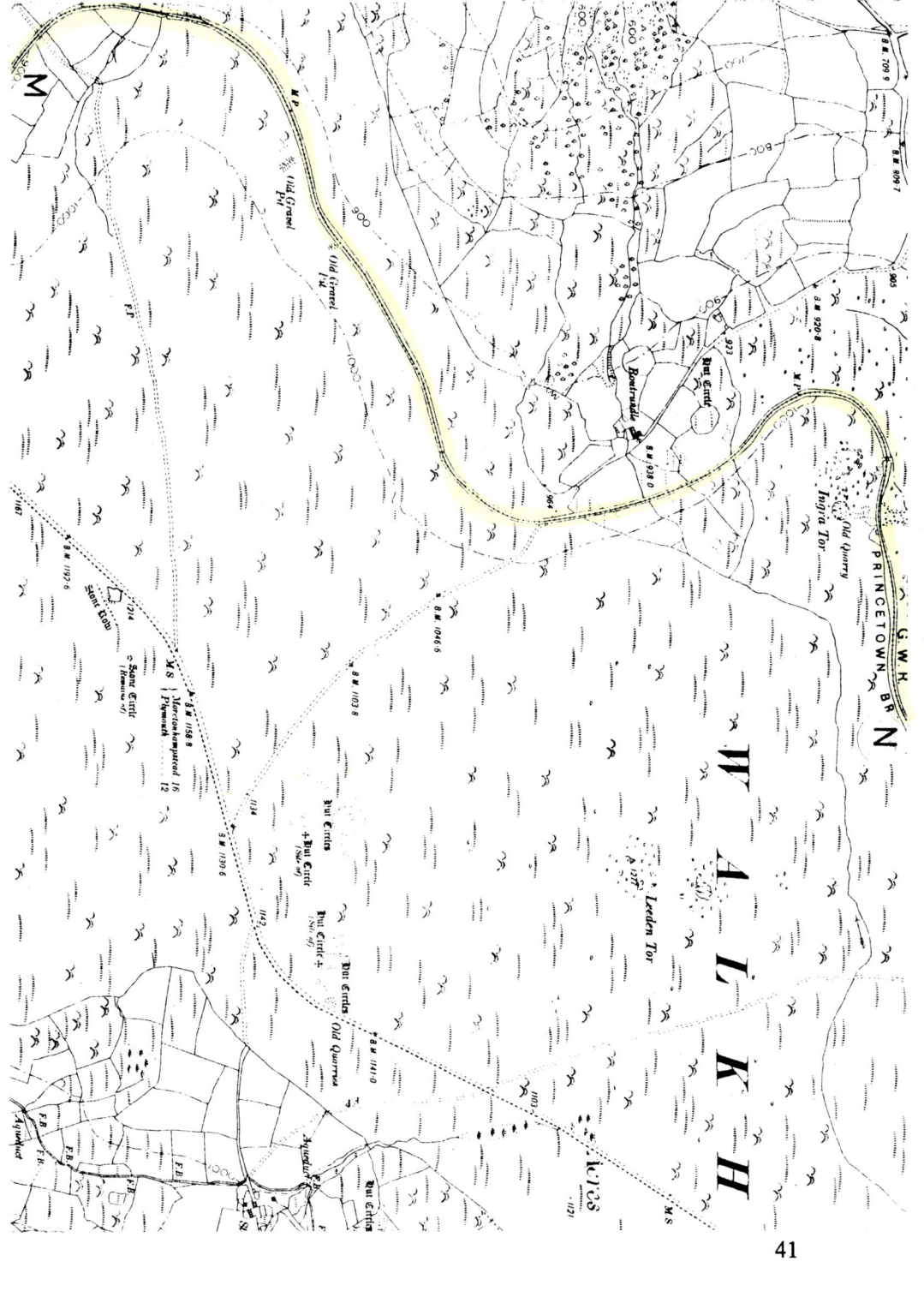

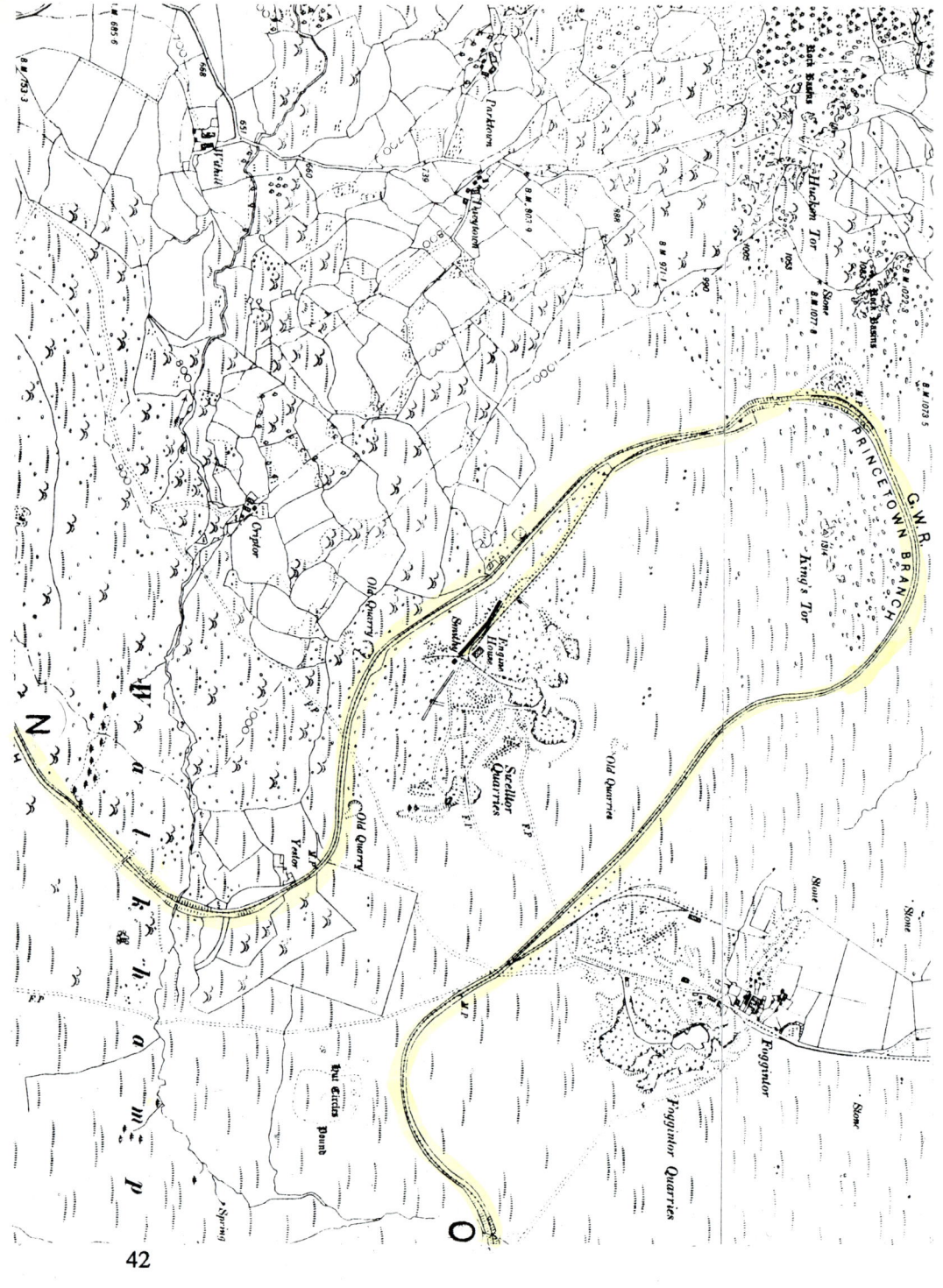

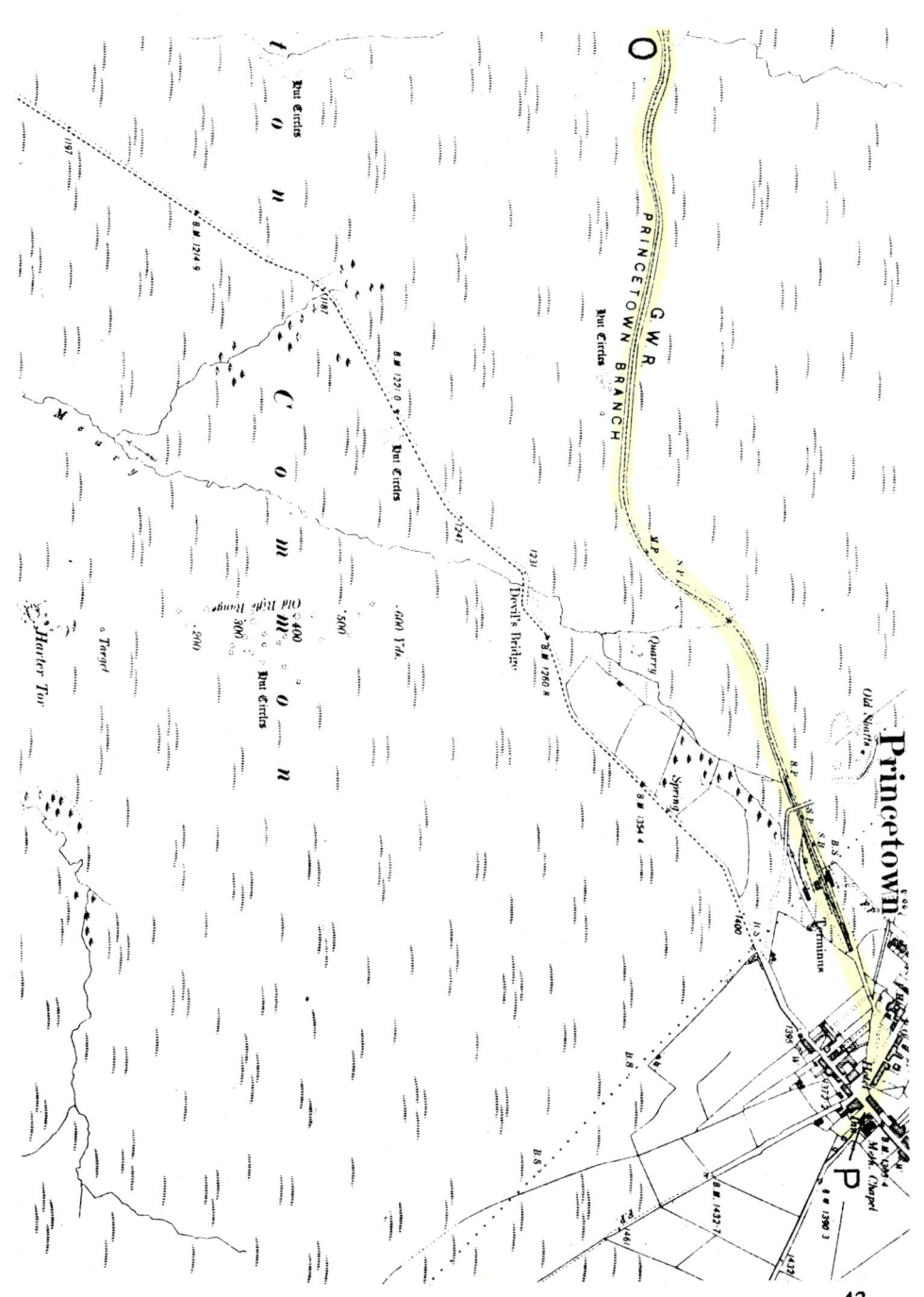

The Lee Moor Tramway (above Plym Bridge)

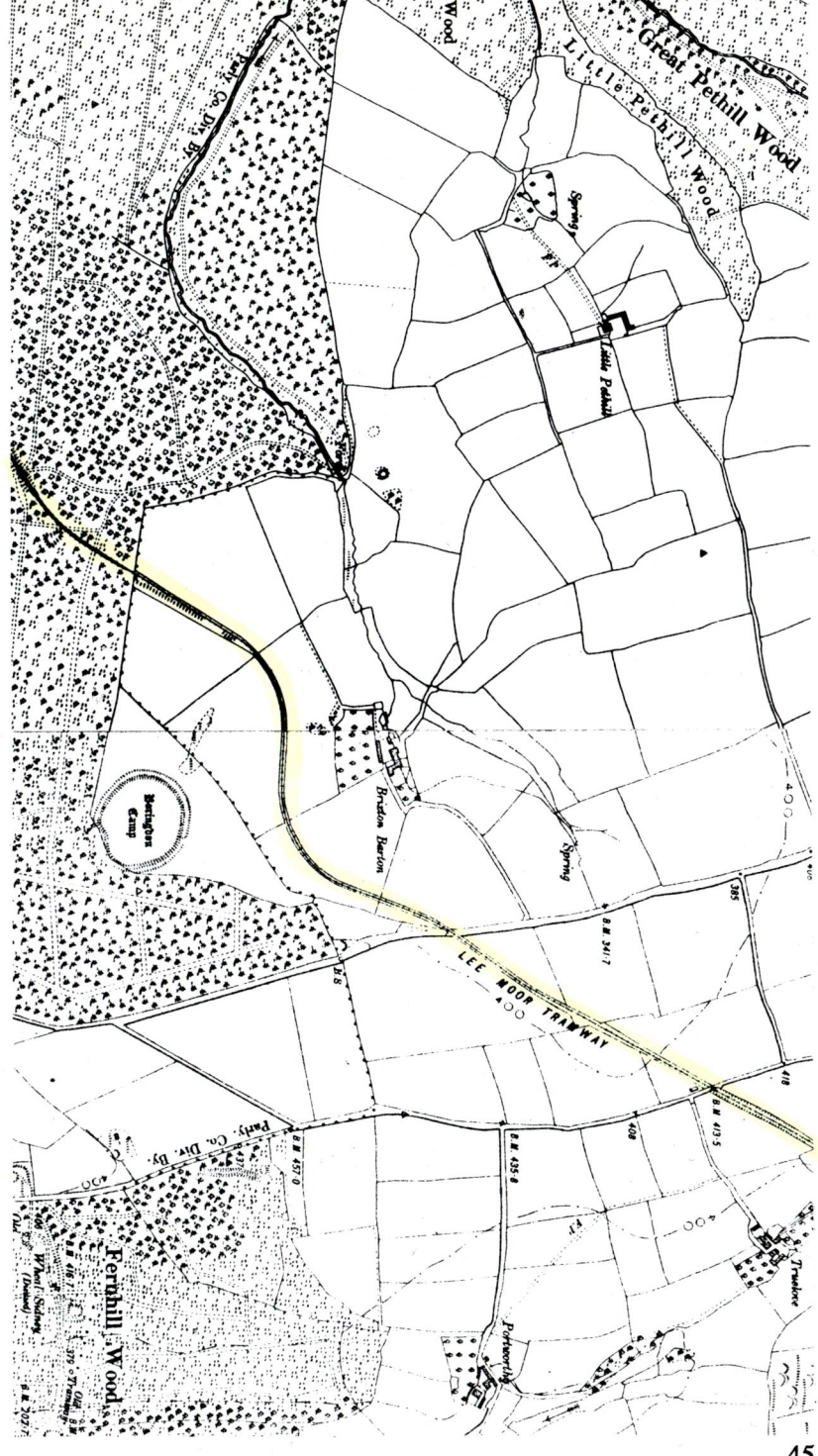

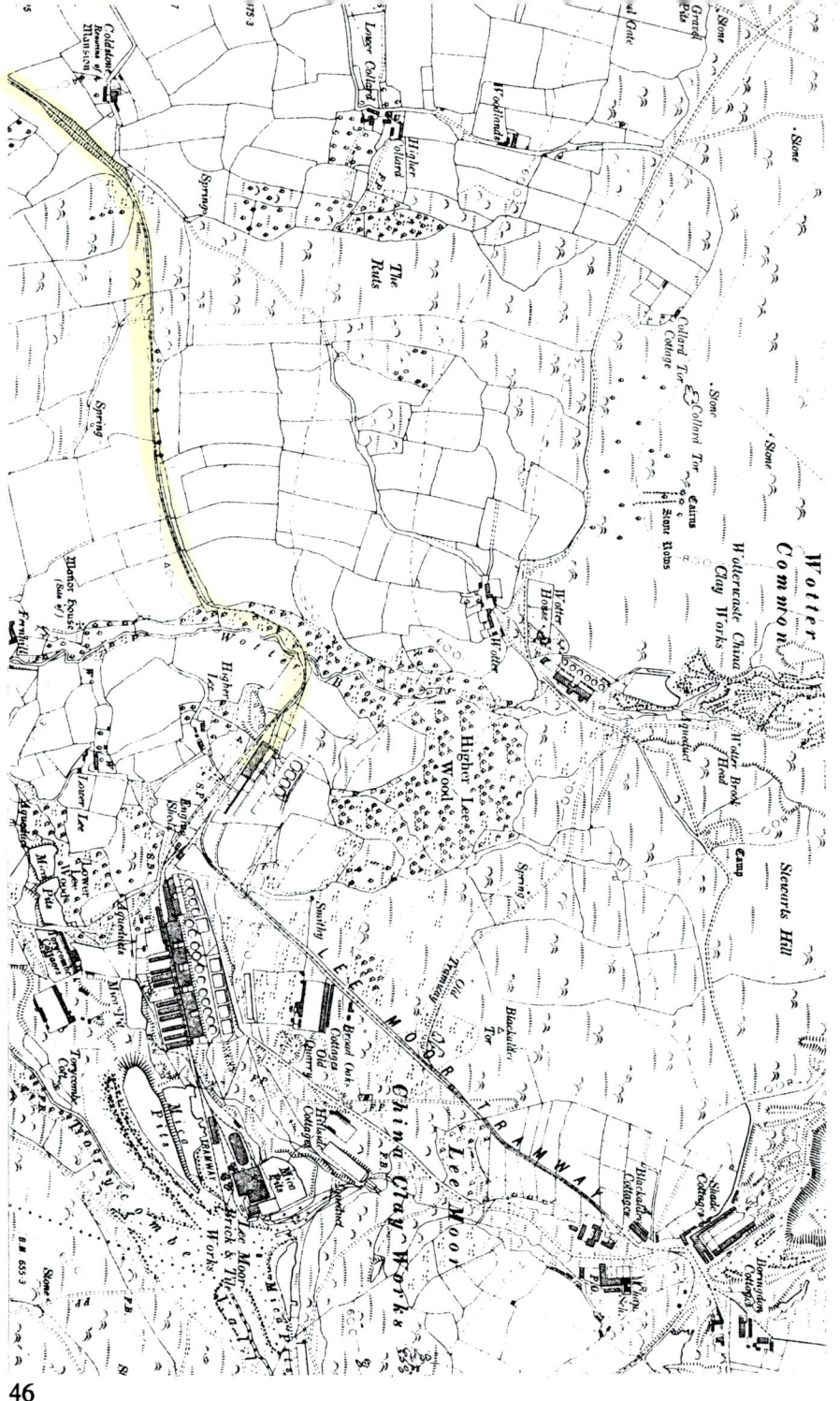

THE PLYMOUTH & DARTMOOR RAILWAY AND THE LEE MOOR TRAMWAY – A SHORT HISTORY

The principal figure in the moves to construct the first, and longest, portion of these railways was Sir Thomas Tyrwhitt. The son of a rector, he was born in Essex in August 1762, was educated at Eton and Christ Church (Oxford), and first developed an interest in Dartmoor after being appointed secretary to the Council of the Prince of Wales.

Before any idea of a railway came about, however, Tyrwhitt set out on an ambitious campaign to bring Dartmoor into cultivation by starting work on building a country house and estate near Two Bridges, which he named Tor Royal. This was in 1785, and over the years that followed he not only went on to enclose a considerable area of land for agricultural purposes but also founded the settlement of Prince's Town (Princetown), where cottages – and an inn – were built for the labourers. In 1796 Tyrwhitt was also elected member of Parliament for Okehampton, a position that he was to occupy until 1802.

Despite strenuous efforts and the investment of large sums of money, Tyrwhitt's plans for the cultivation and development of the moor ultimately failed to come up to expectations, the poverty of the soil and the adverse climate of the area being prime factors. As a result, he began searching for other ways in which to ensure the future of Princetown and, shortly after Britain had resumed war with France in 1803, made successful representations to the Government for a war prison to be built there. This was to provide a means of housing growing numbers of French prisoners who were being incarcerated in hulks near Plymouth, and who were suffering badly from unsanitary and overcrowded conditions.

After the necessary plans had been prepared, the work of building the prison commenced in 1806 (the same year that Tyrwhitt, who laid the foundation stone, was elected member of Parliament for Plymouth) and continued until the end of 1808, using granite from local quarries and moorstone. It was then opened early in the following year, when the first prisoners were marched up from Plymouth to continue their period of confinement. This, in turn, brought a measure of trade and expansion to the village, which was further enhanced when American prisoners of war started arriving at the prison in 1812. Some 3 years later, however, all hostilities ceased with the result that the prison soon became deserted and Princetown, itself, entered a period of rapid decline.

Rather than becoming disillusioned over this state of affairs, the indefatigable Tyrwhitt (now Sir Thomas, after having received the honour of a knighthood in 1812) responded by thinking of other means of bringing prosperity to the area and, on 3rd November 1818, made a proposal to the Plymouth Chamber of Commerce that a railway should be constructed between Princetown and Plymouth. Now this was a bold step indeed as at that time there were no railways of any length in Devon, only some short local lines such as those connected with the building of the Plymouth Breakwater (1812) and with the

Tavistock Canal, at Morwellham (1817). Anyhow, the purpose of the new railway was to assist in the reclamation and cultivation of the areas of Dartmoor "lying barren, desolate and neglected" by transporting lime and sea sand to improve the land, to carry timber for use in the construction of new buildings, which would be built near the railway, and to bring coal and other domestic requirements necessary for the 'colonists' who were to be employed in reclaiming the land. In addition, it was envisaged that products from the moor, itself, such as granite, peat, ores from the mines, together with flax and hemp raised by the proposed agricultural policy, would all be carried on the railway to the quays at Plymouth.

Much to Sir Thomas's delight, the Plymouth Chamber of Commerce accepted the proposal for such a railway to be constructed almost immediately, and a survey of the route of the line was made by William Shillabeer – the schoolmaster at nearby Walkhampton, who was also employed, on a part-time basis, as a surveyor by local landowner Sir Masseh Lopes. This was then followed, on 30th November 1818, by plans being deposited with the Clerk of the Peace for Devon so as to enable a Bill to be presented to the 1819 session of Parliament which, if approved, would authorise the building of the railway. In the meantime, of course, Sir Thomas had to consider the financial implications of his proposed scheme, which led to an initial meeting of persons invited to be subscribers being held in Plymouth on 24th March 1819, and to the formation of a provisional committee consisting of several prominent local personages, including Sir Masseh Lopes, Sir William Elford and Edmund Lockyer. Thereafter, more meetings quickly followed, one of which involved the election of a formal committee (on 20th May 1819) and another, held in June, the discussion of an estimate of £27,783 for the construction of the line received from William Stuart: he, at that time, was the engineer in charge of the building of the Plymouth Breakwater and had been allowed to advise on the railway by the Lords Commissioners of the Admiralty.

The next major development occurred on 2nd July 1819 when the Act of Incorporation of the Plymouth & Dartmoor Railway Company (59 Geo. III, Cap. 115) received Royal Assent. It authorised a share capital of £27,783 (the figure in Stuart's submission) in shares of £50, with power to raise a further £5,000 by additional shares or mortgage, and it now seemed that the greatest obstacle as regards the construction of the railway had been overcome. Indeed, Sir Thomas waited only until 12th August 1819 before ceremonially laying the first rail at Laira. The proceedings, though, must have been initiated merely to advertise and stimulate interest in the undertaking as tenders for the line had still to be accepted at this latter date. In fact, contrary to the hopes and expectations expressed at the first General Meeting of the proprietors to be held in Plymouth on 20th September 1819, with Sir Thomas in the Chair, another 4 years were to elapse before the first part of the line was officially opened for traffic due to a series of unforeseen difficulties. Of course, at this point, it needs to be borne in mind that railways were a new form of transport when the line was first proposed and that none of the persons on the original committee would have had any experience of the practicalities, financial or otherwise, of the running of a railway. Suffice to say, these facts all contributed to many complex negotiations surrounding its authorisation, construction and operation, of which a full account is not considered practical.

Tenders for the construction of the line, initially from Crabtree to Princetown, via Jump (Roborough), and for the supply of rails, were submitted by Messrs. Hugh McIntosh of London and by William Bailey & Co. (also of London) respectively. The committee, meanwhile, enquired of Sir Masseh Lopes as to the charge he would levy for a lease to work granite at Walkhampton Common, an area through which the line was to pass. His reply stated that a royalty of 2d per ton would be levied, but no limit was specified as to the quantities of granite to be removed. The committee, however, felt that the actual excavation of the granite was not a function which they could undertake, and suggested that a private firm could act in conjunction with their company to work the proposed quarries.

Another matter which came under consideration was the fact that the proposed southern terminus of the railway was to be at a small creek at Crabtree, in the Plym estuary, which was some distance from the sea and usable only at times of high tide. A Bill was therefore promoted to extend the line to Sutton Harbour, where loading times would not be so restricted, and this became law on 8th July 1820 (1 Geo. IV, Cap. 54), the cost of the work being £7,200. An additional extension was to lead to a wharf on the Cattewater in the lower reaches of the Plym estuary.

In the years leading up to the building of the Plymouth & Dartmoor Railway another project was already in progress, namely the construction of the Plymouth Breakwater, for which large quantities of stone were required. The firm of Johnson and Bryse held a contract for supplying granite to surface the breakwater, and the news that large quantities might be available in the near future, with a means of transport to Plymouth, prompted them to approach the railway committee with an offer to pay two shillings and six pence per ton for the carriage of granite for a period of 7 years, subject to an average of 8,000 tons per annum. The committee welcomed this proposed source of traffic as providing a guaranteed income, and signed an Agreement with Johnson and Bryse on 21st September 1820. Meanwhile, although the estimated cost of the construction of the railway (£27,783) had already been fully subscribed by April 1820, it was decided to apply to the Exchequer Loans Commissioners for a loan of £10,000 so as to avoid excessive annual calls on the subscribers. It subsequently transpired, however, that the cost of purchasing the necessary lands for the railway greatly exceeded the original estimates, and accordingly it was agreed to amend the amount requested from the Exchequer Loans Commissioners to £18,000. This additional sum was perhaps the first sign that the financial situation of the Company was to be far from satisfactory and, indeed, the subsequent history of the railway presents a melancholy picture of insufficient revenue and outstanding loans. It would seem also that members of the committee were beginning to realise the financial implications of the scheme as in August 1820 there were numerous absentees from the meetings; nevertheless, it was agreed that William Stuart be appointed to take over the entire superintendance of the construction works.

By now, the tender of William Bailey for the supply of iron rails had already been accepted (April 1820), as had those for the construction of the formation (June 1820), initially as far as Jump (Roborough) and thereafter for the remainder of the route to Princetown; although no precise date is recorded, construction would have commenced in that year. The track laid in the initial construction consisted of cast-iron fish-bellied rails laid on stone sleepers, each rail being butt-jointed to the next in the chairs. The rails had a maximum depth of 6 inches and a length of 2 feet 10 inches, whilst the railway, itself, consisted of a single line of rails, with sidings (or 'turnouts') at intervals. Some sidings were laid with dressed granite instead of cast-iron rails.

The line was planned as a 'turnpike' railway in that persons using it would be charged rates for the distance travelled and the tonnage carried.

At the end of 1820 William Stuart reported that gradients which had been surveyed on the portion of the line between Crabtree and Jump, via Fursdon, were too severe for horse-drawn trains, and suggested measures that could be taken to remedy the situation. The committee, however, felt that the blame for this serious error lay with Stuart, even though the original survey had been made by William Shillabeer, and appointed Roger Hopkins of Swansea (who was later to be involved with the construction of the Bodmin & Wadebridge Railway) as assistant engineer. The outcome was a proposal for an alternative route which included a tunnel at Leigham, and several miles through the valley of the River Plym, some distance to the east of the original survey. The estimate for this unforeseen work was £5,000 and an Act authorising its construction became law on 2nd July 1821 (1&2 Geo. IV, Cap. 125).

This new route passed through land owned by the Earl of Morley, and a condition of his approval to the scheme was that his slatestone quarry at Cann should be connected to the railway; this condition was accepted apparently without reference to the full committee, and an undertaking signed by three members to the effect that a connection would be provided either by an inclined plane or 'branch' railway. The construction of the main railway to Princetown was in progress at this time, but no works were commenced to link the Earl's quarry as matters were not running smoothly for the railway company: William Stuart was in dispute with the committee concerning his alleged erroneous survey of the route, and was dismissed from his position of Engineer in October 1821, whilst the contractor building the railway, Hugh McIntosh, was replaced by Johnson and Bryse (who were now operating as Johnson Bros.) in June 1822, after a disagreement and arbitration regarding the standard of the line's construction!

The building of the railway continued under the supervision of Roger Hopkins and a modified form of rail was brought into use which was of the same fish-bellied type, but with a length of 3 feet 10 inches and having lapped instead of butt-joints. The line was almost completed by the summer of 1823 and a public notice issued on 19th September of that year stated that Opening Day would be one week later, on 26th September 1823.

The day commenced with a breakfast given by Sir Thomas Tyrwhitt at his wharf on Roborough Down, "where marquees were erected and every elegant species of viand provided". It has been stated that the 'wharf' was the building which still stands by the route of the line above Clearbrook, but a booklet entitled *Buckland Monachorum*, which was compiled by a Miss Alice Bere for the Womens Institute and published around 1930, includes a short description of the railway. This makes the statement that the breakfast was given "to a large company at what is now part of the Rock Hotel, which was then the office and warehouse for the granite". This, of course, refers to the wharf at Yelverton and is confirmed by a further statement that "an isolated building on the moor near Clearbrook is said to have been one of the stables for the tram horses". The celebrations, themselves, were dampened by unfavourable weather, but a long file of 'cars' carrying granite, stewards and other individuals (accompanied by a band) set off for Plymouth, which was finally reached at 7p.m. after what must have been a very protracted and tiring journey.

Following the celebrations at the opening of the railway, it soon became clear that apart from the granite from the quarries on Walkhampton Common there was little or no other traffic. Nevertheless, the extensions at each end of the line – to Sutton Pool in the south and to Princetown in the north – were completed in December 1825 and December 1826 respectively. The contractor in each case was again Johnson Bros. but, as the railway company had no finance to settle their account, the tolls which had been agreed for the carriage of the granite were set against the construction costs; consequently, the Johnsons had virtually a private railway for their granite. In addition, the railway company had not repaid the loan from the Exchequer Loans Commissioners, while another problem concerned the promised connection to the Earl of Morley's slatestone quarry – it had not yet been built! Moreover, in spite of renewed pressure from the Earl, it was not until 1829 that the work was finally completed. Then, at long last, a line left the Plymouth & Dartmoor's main line near the Rising Sun Inn at Crabtree and ran to the terminal basin of a canal, which His Lordship had constructed from Cann Quarry to Marsh Mills. The opening date is variously recorded as 20th November 1829 or 20th January 1830 and, at that time, the line was half a mile in length. In 1833, however, it was extended for a further 2 miles, being laid along the towpath of the canal (which then reverted to a mill leat), passing Plym Bridge and entering directly into the quarry workings.

The year 1833 was also eventful for two other reasons. Firstly, it saw the passing of Sir Thomas Tyrwhitt, who died on 24th February with his dreams of the development of Dartmoor largely unrealised. Secondly, Lord Morley, who held mineral rights on land at Lee Moor, signed an Agreement with the Johnson brothers on 23rd July for the building of a further branch line from Marsh Mills to a wharf near St. Mary's Church at Plympton. The idea here was to enable china clay from the workings at Lee Moor (which had been leased to J & W Phillips) to be brought down by pack-horses to Plympton, then transferred to the railway. Opened sometime in 1834, the line concerned was a mile long.

Interestingly enough, the original intention had been to extend this particular line up the valley of the Tory Brook to the Lee Moor area. This, of course, would then have dispensed with the need for pack-horses, but the owner of Newnham Park refused permission for any construction across his land, with the result that the extension was never built. Even so, it did nothing to detract from the fact that the railway was now carrying clay and slatestone, in addition to large amounts of granite from the moorland quarries. These quarries, incidentally, were providing employment for several hundred men, some of whom were accommodated in a group of cottages which had been erected at Foggintor.

The next important stage in the history of the Plymouth & Dartmoor Railway came in the years immediately following 1840. Already moves were afoot by the Bristol & Exeter Railway Company to extend its broad-gauge line to Exeter, and in 1843 the South Devon Railway Company deposited a Bill for a further extension of the route from Exeter to Plymouth. Initially, this latter aspect appeared to be of no great significance so far as the Plymouth & Dartmoor Railway was concerned, but later it was realised that part of the proposed route severed the Plympton branch near its eastern terminus. This then produced a series of objections from the Plymouth & Dartmoor Railway Committee – during which it emerged that in reality John and William Johnson were now 'in possession' of the railway! That, of course, was a completely different matter, and one that would eventually lead to the election of a new committee. But, in the meantime, the objections failed to prevent the Bill from receiving Royal Assent, thereby allowing the branch to be sold to the South Devon Railway Company. Its closure then followed in 1847, thus permitting the new main-line railway to reach Laira Green, on the outskirts of Plymouth, in May 1848.

Needless to say, the closure of the Plympton branch now meant that the china clay works at Lee Moor no longer had rail access to the wharves at Plymouth. As a result, a Plympton surveyor named John Andrew was asked to produce plans for an alternative line that would connect to the Cann Quarry Railway near Plym Bridge. At around the same time, though, the idea of another new 'main line' railway – from Marsh Mills to Tavistock – was being mooted, which ultimately led to the proposed scheme being shelved. Instead, after the South Devon & Tavistock Railway had been promoted in 1852, Lord Morley, who owned part of the land through which the line was to pass, and who was by then chairman of the provisional board of directors, made it a condition of his support of the railway that a 'branch' line be constructed to reach Lee Moor. In reality, this meant an extension of the Cann Quarry Railway from near Plym Bridge as proposed soon after the closure of the Plympton branch!

Acceptance of the condition imposed by Lord Morley was obviously soon forthcoming as on 5th July 1852 he was invited to sign an Agreement between himself, The Lee Moor Porcelain Co and the lessee of the clay works, William Phillips, of the one part and the South Devon and the South Devon & Tavistock Railway Companies of the other part. Included in this Agreement was a stipulation that Lord Morley would give possession of land for the Lee Moor line, at agricultural value, to the South Devon & Tavistock Railway Company, which, in turn, would appoint a contractor to build the 'branch' line within 6 months of acquiring the land.

In the event the work commenced in September 1852, but a formal contract was not signed with the contractors, Messrs Hutchinson and Ritson, until 15th February 1853. They were then required to complete the construction at a cost of £7,150 by 1st May 1853. Not surprisingly, this proved to be an impossible task, and trial working was not in progress until August 1854. Moreover, the end result was far from satisfactory. It was, in fact, so bad as to be unsafe due to many instances of shoddy workmanship, the worst example being the timber viaduct over the Wotter Brook on the approach to Torycombe – this had a length of 627 feet instead of the specified 700 feet! Both self-acting inclines were considered unusable, and an accident at Cann Wood in October 1854 led to the suspension of traffic over the line. William Phillips, who had required early completion of the line in order to transport his clay by rail, then found that because of its condition, the South Devon & Tavistock Railway Company refused to honour its agreement to work the line, and would not carry out the necessary improvements to put it in safe working order. This resulted in the clay having to be carted to Plym Bridge once more prior to being transferred to the Cann Quarry branch.

The Act of Incorporation of the South Devon & Tavistock Railway (of 7ft 0^{1}/4 in. gauge) had finally received Royal Assent in July 1854, but in June 1856 the company rid itself of the Lee Moor line by paying off the contractor and making a gift of it to Lord Morley. Phillips then carried out an overhaul of the line; work which included attending to the proper completion of the Wotter viaduct, the building of a new winding house for the Cann Wood incline and a completely new alignment of the Torycombe incline. Even so, it was not until 24th September 1858 that the tramway, as it had become known, could finally be opened, when a special ceremony to mark the occasion was held in the presence of the Earl and Countess of Morley and other prominent local personages. The permanent way at that time, incidentally, consisted of 'T'-section rails jointed in chairs and secured with metal keys, the whole being laid on stone sleeper blocks. At this point, it also needs to be recorded that just beforehand, in June, Lord Morley had leased both the Lee Moor Tramway and the Cann Quary line to Phillips for a term of 999 years.

It was during the 1850s that two other developments occurred relevant to the history of the railways. Firstly, the branch to Sutton Pool was purchased by the South Devon Railway Company in 1851, converted to mixed gauges of 4ft. 6in. and 7ft. $0^{1}/4$ in. and re-opened in 1853 (still with horse traction) prior to improvements being carrried out to the route in the years 1856 – 1857. Secondly, the Cann Quarry branch was closed to regular traffic above Plym Bridge in 1855, although the rails were not removed.

Returning now to the original railway, the Plymouth & Dartmoor Company was reconstituted in 1865 by an Act of Parliament (28–9 Vic., Cap. 131) whereby William Johnson, who had taken over the mortgages on the railway held by the Commissioners for the issue of Exchequer Bills, was to receive preference shares in the sum of £75,000; this, in reality, constituted the purchase price of the line by the new company. Being now freed from the domination of the Johnson influence, the railway continued to carry granite and china clay and, in 1870, the tolls that had been received to date enabled the company to declare a small dividend – the first ever! Later, in the years 1873 and 1874, money also became available to purchase 600 tons of rails, which were used to repair the line. In the meantime, another significant development took place on the branch to Sutton Pool when, in 1869, the 4ft. 6in. rails were removed from the mixed gauge section and locomotive traction was introduced on the broad-gauge rails. This, in turn, left only the wharf on the Cattewater for the horse-drawn trains of the earlier 4ft. 6in. gauge.

Before long even greater changes were looming. The first signs of these came in March of 1877 when the Great Western Railway (now in possession of the South Devon & Tavistock Railway) considered a proposal for a branch line that would make a connection to Princetown. In the event, this was not proceeded with, as later in the year the Plymouth & Dartmoor Railway Company made an offer to sell the portion of its line from near Yelverton to Princetown in return for £22,000 worth of shares in the new railway, most of the length of which would be laid on the track-bed of the existing line. Plans were then deposited on 30th November 1877, and the Bill promoting the new line received Royal Assent on 13th August 1878. However, it was not until 11th August 1883 that it was finally opened for traffic – just 2 days before the 5-year limit in the Act of 1878 was due to expire!

Deprived of its main source of revenue, the carrying of granite, the section of the old Plymouth & Dartmoor Railway between Yelverton and the junction with the Lee Moor Tramway at Crabtree then fell into disuse. The actual rails, though, remained in situ until 1916, when they were finally lifted, together with those of the Cann Quarry line above Plym Bridge, so as to provide metal for munitions during World War I. Meanwhile, with closure occurring on the northern end of the system, the only portion left in operation was that used by the Lee Moor Tramway, the route of which included the remaining sections of the Cann Quarry and Marsh Mills lines, together with the original Plymouth & Dartmoor route from Crabtree to the Cattewater. This remaining portion, incidentally, now crossed other railways – the Plymouth to Tavistock line, the main line from Paddington (at Laira), the Yealmpton branch and the Cattewater branch – on the level at four locations.

Prior to all these developments, the lease of the Lee Moor clay works had been transferred (in 1862) from the Phillips family to Mrs R. Martin, and this had resulted in the terminus on the Cattewater becoming known as Martin's Wharf. Of far greater significance, however, was the fact that with traffic having continued to increase on the tramway, it was eventually decided to introduce steam traction on the section from Torycombe to the Cann Wood incline, the track here being relaid with heavier rail prior to the delivery of two locomotives in 1899. It was also around this time that changes in production were to bring about the demise of the Wotter branch, which was closed during the following year. Later, the section of track from Lee Moor village to Cholwichtown was destined to suffer the same fate for similar reasons.

In 1919 the English China Clay Company took over the Lee Moor workings and tramway, and then, following a merger in 1932, the operations came under the control of English Clays, Lovering Pochin and Co. Meanwhile, the tramway continued to carry china clay to the Laira transfer sidings or to Martin's Wharf right up until the outbreak of World War II, although the

A train arriving at Torycombe on 18th August 1939, hauled by 0–4–0ST 'LEE MOOR No 2'.

Torycombe incline and the section of track leading to Lee Moor village was not used beyond 1936. Another development had been the laying of a pipe-line to carry liquid china clay from Lee Moor to a processing works at Marsh Mills, with direct access to the Great Western Railway.

Following the outbreak of war, the production of china clay from Lee Moor was reduced. This, combined with the fact that by now ever-increasing amounts of liquid china clay were being conveyed through the pipe-line, saw the use of the tramway fall steadily into decline, even though some additional traffic was generated by materials needing to be transported for storage from Devonport Dockyard. Nevertheless, operation of the tramway continued at least until 1944, as a visit in March of that year revealed; the rails at Torycombe showed signs of recent use and loaded wagons were standing in the sidings. The precise date of the cessation of traffic is not known, but there are a number of factors that indicate that it was most probably at the end of 1945. Firstly, an article in the *Western Morning News* on 20th October 1961 stated that the locomotives had then been in 'honourable retirement' for 16 years (i.e. from 1945). Secondly, Mr. F. Sercombe, an employee of the clay company who returned from service in the Armed Forces in early 1946, stated that the tramway was already out of use by that date. Thirdly, the last person to drive the engines, the late Mr. George Poynter, informed members of the Lee Moor Tramway Preservation Society that the last occasion on which a locomotive (No. 2) was put in steam was 31st December 1945.

A further visit made at the beginning of March 1947 revealed that at that time the tramway had certainly been disused for a considerable period. The two locomotives were locked inside their shed at Torycombe, a semi-derelict, loaded wagon stood on the rails immediately outside and several of the lines in the area were becoming buried. In addition, two more loaded wagons stood on the Wotter curve, where one of the rails of the 'main' line had disappeared beneath a thick layer of mould and fallen leaves, whilst farther down the line, near the head of the Cann Wood incline, a fallen tree lay across the track.

Although the tramway was no longer being used to transport china clay, the owning company had not finally decided on its abandonment. Instead, it was left in 'suspended animation' for several years, with the rolling stock standing at various locations. In fact, in May 1955 there were thirty-four wagons and two rail-mounted cranes in the transfer sidings at Laira, seven more wagons in a siding near the bridge over the River Plym near Marsh Mills, a further eighteen in Truelove cutting, four on the 'main' line near the Wotter curve and eight in sidings at Torycombe, making a total of seventy-one wagons in all. There were also some more wagons in the works sidings beyond the level-crossing at Torycombe. Many retained number plates, the highest seen being No. 138.

During the following month (June 1955) the wagons in Truelove cutting were moved nearer to Lee Moor and the track lifted here so as to permit the laying of a new clay pipe-line. Also, in the same month, a small diversion of the tramway was made at the entrance to an engineering works just to the east

Disused wagons and rail-mounted cranes standing in the transfer sidings at Laira on 24th August 1955.

of the level-crossing over the A38 near the Rising Sun Inn. Although the line was now out of use, it was considered necessary, in case at some future date it should again be brought back into use, to maintain the right of way on the lower section, and in particular over the level-crossing with the main line from Paddington at Laira. For that purpose, occasional short horse-drawn trains were operated to convey sand from a loading ramp and siding near Weighbridge Cottage, at Marsh Mills, to Maddock's Concrete Works, which adjoined the line near the southern end of the Embankment. However, of the seven wagons in the Marsh Mills siding, only two, Nos. 27 and 54, remained serviceable by 1954 to carry this traffic.

In 1960 the clay company made a final decision to abandon the tramway, resulting in the withdrawal of the sand trains; the last trip, consisting of a horse drawing a single wagon, was made on 26th August 1960. Thus, after 137 years, the horse-drawn trains of South-West Devon became a thing of the past. Following the closure, the level-crossing over the main line from Paddington at Laira was removed in October/November 1960, whilst all the wagons were scrapped and much of the track from Torycombe to near Marsh Mills was lifted in 1961, making way for a new clay pipe-line. Most of the remaining track was removed in the following summer. The dismantling of the tramway and the scrapping of the rolling stock did not, however, include the two locomotives, and they remained securely locked in their shed, where they had stood since 1946.

Having completed the account of the construction and operation of the Plymouth & Dartmoor Railway and its associated lines, it must be mentioned that the Company was also involved with obtaining Parliamentary powers to build some of the later railways in the Plymouth area, which were not part of the 4ft. 6in. gauge system. These included:–

(a) An Act of 19 July 1875 (38–9 Vic., Cap. 154) for a line to connect the L & SWR with the Cattewater, which was worked under agreement by the L & SWR.

(b) An Act of 2 August 1883 (46–7 Vic., Cap. 139) for a line from Laira to Turnchapel, also worked by the L & SWR.

(c) An Act of 28 June 1888 (51–2 Vic., Cap. 53) for a line from Plymstock to Yealmpton and Modbury, which was worked by the GWR as far as Yealmpton; the Modbury extension was never built.

An interesting feature concerning the Turnchapel line appears in the documents of sale of Pomphlett Tide Water Grist Mill at Plymstock, which were issued in 1922. These stated that two small portions of the mill pool had been taken 'for the purposes of the P&D.R.' in the construction of an embankment for the Turnchapel line and the Company was required to pay £0–17–8 (88p) per annum for Fee Farm Rent, and to maintain two culverts under the embankment.

The end of the story is that the Plymouth & Dartmoor Railway Company was incorporated into the group of companies forming the Southern Railway under the provisions of the Railway Act of 1921, thus terminating its separate existence after a little over a century.

THE PLYMOUTH & DARTMOOR RAILWAY – ROLLING STOCK

As stated elsewhere, the original intention of the promoters of the Plymouth & Dartmoor Railway was to construct a line which would be used to transport commodities of many varieties to and from the moorland area. It appears, therefore, that open wagons, possibly similar to those operating in later years on the Lee Moor Tramway, must have formed part of the rolling stock, particularly when the later 'branch' lines were opened to traffic. Precise details of these early wagons are not known, but a description of the wagons used to transport large blocks of stone from the quarries is given in an account written by two German mining engineers who visited the railway in about 1826. It says that these vehicles were constructed with a flat platform surface of wooden planks laid on wooden mainframes with connecting beams, the planks being reinforced with iron bars. There were no springs, the bearings for the axles being in wooden blocks below the mainframe beams. The wheels were of cast iron, and ran loose on the axles, whilst brakes were fitted to both wheels on one side. In addition, to enable the large blocks of stone to be moved and loaded in the quarries, one vehicle was converted to carry a crane with a rotating wooden jib.

None of these wagons has survived, but the description gives a picture of a wagon very similar to those used on the Merchants Railway on the Isle of Portland. This line, opened in 1826 and of the same gauge (4ft. 6in.), was also used to transport large blocks of stone from quarries; it remained in use until 1939.

One person who had first hand knowledge of the riding of the flat wagons was that great authority on Dartmoor, the late William Crossing, who was born in 1847. In his work entitled *Presentday Life on Dartmoor* (later published in book form as *Crossing's Dartmoor Worker*), he states that he had ridden on the tram wagons frequently "both when laden with granite or when returning to the quarries empty, and, cumbrous though they were, they ran smoothly enough". The railway and the area of the granite quarries were also visited, in 1831, by the Reverend E. A. Bray. He, at that time, was Vicar of Tavistock and writes of seeing on the railway at the quarries "a rude kind of vis-a-vis with an awning". This indicates a type of vehicle for the purpose of carrying passengers, with seats facing each other, and he assumed such were used to bring pleasure parties from Plymouth. It is possible that this was, indeed, the case, as no doubt the railway company would have been anxious to augment its income by any means at its disposal. An alternative explanation could, perhaps, be that it was an early form of Directors' inspection carriage, similar to the vehicle used on the Portreath Tramway in Cornwall.

THE LEE MOOR TRAMWAY – ROLLING STOCK

The Lee Moor Tramway was built for the purpose of conveying china clay and other products from the works in the Lee Moor area down to navigable water, or to the main line railway system, in the Plymouth area. Apart from a small number of special-purpose vehicles, the rolling stock consisted of four-wheeled, three-plank, wooden-bodied wagons with dumb buffers and side chains. A central draw-bar with coupling pin ran from end to end below the body and was used when the wagons were attached to the incline cables or being hauled on the locomotive-worked section of the tramway. A hand-brake was fitted on one side and operated on both wheels. Each wagon could carry a payload of around 3 tons of clay.

Wagons loaded with casks of clay at the lower end of the Cann Wood incline c1920.
F. H. C. Casbourn, courtesy of The Stephenson Locomotive Society

Large numbers of the wagons were constructed in the clay company's workshops at Lee Moor, but an early batch was built for the tramway by Charles Roberts & Co. of Wakefield. The majority of the rolling stock ran on wheels fixed to the axles, but a small number built at Lee Moor were fitted with wheels which ran loose on the axles. These wagons had roller-bearings, which ran freely, but were not entirely successful as the axles tended to fracture when operating on the inclines. At its maximum, the fleet numbered about 140, but at the time of closure this had been reduced to almost half of that figure. Initially painted a dull red, in later years the wagons were unpainted and were stained to a greyish white colour by the loads of clay which they carried. Number plates were fitted, cast in iron or, in some cases,

A wagon photographed by the level-crossing at Torycombe.
F. H. C. Casbourn, courtesy of The Stephenson Locomotive Society

Water tank wagons used for balancing the weight of trains on the Torycombe incline.
F. H. C. Casbourn, courtesy of The Stephenson Locomotive Society

in lead. One end of the body could be opened for loading and unloading, being hung on a hinge at the top, whilst a section of one side was similarly hinged at the base.

On the Cann Wood incline, the weight of the descending train was more than sufficient to counterbalance the ascending one, but this was not always the case on the Torycombe incline. Here, in order to provide the necessary weight on descending trains, several flat wagons were fitted with water tanks and kept at the top of the incline. These were then used if loaded wagons containing coal or other materials were required to be brought up to Lee Moor village or to the various claypits in the neighbourhood. When loaded, each wagon weighed 4 tons, and they were sometimes used in pairs. Two other, special-purpose, vehicles were to be found on the line; these were hand-operated, rail-mounted cranes used to transfer loads between the tramway wagons and standard-gauge wagons in the transfer sidings at Laira.

Although the definition of 'rolling stock' is not appropriate for the horses used to haul the trains, they were an essential part of the tramway throughout its life. There were two main stables, one at Martin's Wharf on the Cattewater and one in the village at Lee Moor, fourteen animals being stabled at either location. A smaller stable was situated beside the track at the lower end of the Cann Wood incline, near Plym Bridge. Each train, made up of three, four or five wagons, was hauled by a pair of the horses.

At the end of the 19th century, steam locomotives were introduced on the tramway, and served the line successfully for many years. There were two engines, built by Peckett & Sons at their Atlas Works in Bristol. They were of the maker's M4 class as used on standard-gauge lines, but with the wheel tyres modified to suit the slightly narrower gauge of the tramway. Numbered 783 and 784 in their maker's lists, the former was delivered on 24th March 1899 and became 'LEE MOOR No 1', while the second followed on 6th April 1899, being named 'LEE MOOR No 2'. They were 0–4–0 saddle tank locomotives, weighing 13tons 15cwt. (including 2 tons of coal), with coupled wheels 2ft. 6in. in diameter, and a wheelbase of 5ft. Other features included two outside cylinders of 10 in. x 20in., a working boiler pressure of 120lbs per square inch and a tractive effort at a working pressure of 6,800lbs. Braking was by means of a hand-brake at the back of the cab, and tool-boxes and sand-boxes were carried on the running plate on either side. Traversing jacks were provided in case of derailment. The rear sheet of the cabs reached only to waist level, so in order to give the drivers protection from the weather wooden frames, covered with metal sheeting and having two small rectangular spectacles, were provided for both engines.

Early photographs show the engines with their names painted on the saddle tanks, but brass nameplates were subsequently fitted. The livery was lined green, with brass dome covers and safety valves, while the appearance of the engines was further enhanced by copper-capped chimneys. During their working lives, repairs were carried out by Peckett & Sons on a number of occasions; to No 1 in December 1913, September 1926 and October 1932,

'LEE MOOR No 1' shunting at Torycombe.
F. H. C. Casbourn, courtesy of The Stephenson Locomotive Society

and to No 2 in January 1913, February 1928 and November 1935.

The construction of the locomotive shed at Torycombe was brickwork with a tiled roof, sliding doors giving access through an opening at the eastern end. The western opening was filled by corrugated iron sheeting on a wooden framework, the upper portion at each end being of wood, with a window reaching almost to the apex. Each side-wall had two windows, and metal smoke vents in the roof were placed to correspond with the chimneys of the engines, which stood one behind the other on a single track. A brick-lined inspection pit extended almost the whole length of the shed, the rails being laid on longitudinal baulks of timber. Work benches were provided along the side-walls, and a water supply was obtained from a tap sited inside the shed.

ENGINEERING AND OPERATING DATA

(Reproduced from the "Appendix to the No. 6 Section of the Service Time Tables, G.W.R. Plymouth Division – April 1939", courtesy of the National Railway Museum)

Leemoor Transfer Siding.

This Siding is within three feet of a Great Western Siding, and whenever there are any wagons standing in the Great Western Siding, a red flag by day and a red light by night must be hung on the last vehicle to indicate that it is not an Exchange Siding, and that Shunters must not go between the wagons.

YEALMPTON BRANCH.
Mount Gould Junction—Working Tram Wagons over the Dartmoor Tramway.

1. The Dartmoor Tramway passes across the Yealmpton Branch at the junction of the latter with the Sutton Harbour Branch, and Safety Apparatus has been provided to ensure that no obstruction from Tram Wagons shall affect Yealmpton Branch Trains. This has been fixed at the junction of the Yealmpton Branch, and in the Mount Gould Signal Box ; and the Signalman there has control over the arrangement.

The appliances are as follows :—

2. Locking Frame Lever, No. 12.—This lever, when drawn from the back to the front position of the Locking Frame, locks all signals and points leading to or from the Yealmpton Branch, and at the same time is locked itself by the electric lock, and closes two Throw-off points on the Sutton Harbour side, and two on the Laira side of the Yealmpton Branch line.

3. Electric Lock Box.—Immediately behind No. 12 lever, and secured to the floor, is an iron box containing the electric lock. The cover of this Box is padlocked, and the key of the padlock is held by the District Lineman. At the top of this box is the Emergency Lever.

4. Emergency Lever.—This is a small brass lever, standing when in its normal position at an angle of about 45 degrees to the top of the box and padlocked, the Signalman holding the key of the padlock.

When necessary, the Signalman can release this padlock and move the lever to the vertical position and padlock it there, this movement having the effect of switching the electric lock, and consequently the Safety Apparatus out of use.

The key of this padlock must be kept in a place of security where each Signalman in turn can obtain it when wanted.

5. Electric Lock Indicator.—This is placed on a shelf behind No. 12 lever, and its use is to indicate to the Signalman when the electric lock is on or off.

The instrument shows three indications, one at a time, as follows :—

"Lock on"   "Wrong"   "Lock off"
(Red disc)   (Black disc)   (White disc)

When No. 12 lever is in the forward position, the red disc shews
"Lock on."

When No. 12 lever is in the back position, the white disc should shew
"Lock off."
which is the normal indication when the Safety Apparatus is not in use.

Should anything be wrong with the apparatus within the "Electric Lock Box," or the batteries relating thereto, the black disc showing
"Wrong"
will be visible, and the Signalman will then know that the instrument is out of order, and requires attention. If the difficulty be one the Signalman cannot rectify, he must send for the Lineman.

6. Foot Plunger.—In front of No. 12 lever, and projecting only slightly above the floor level is the brass top of the foot plunger, the object of which is to enable the Signalman, by placing his foot upon it, to release the electric Lock from No. 12 lever, so that at the proper moment, which will be described hereafter, he may move that lever from the front to the back position.

7. Fouling Bars and Contact Boxes.—Between the two Throw-off points on the Sutton Harbour side, and the two on the Laira side of the Yealmpton Branch, flat bars of iron, counterweighted, are placed close to, and parallel with, one rail of the Tramway.

These flat bars are continuous, but made in several sections, and each section is coupled to a "Contact Box" placed by the side of the Tramway.

Yealmpton Branch—*continued.*

Mount Gould Junction—Working Tram Wagons over the Dartmoor Tramway.—*continued.*

8. The mode of procedure for passing Tram Wagons and using the Safety Apparatus, is as follows :—

When a train of Tram Wagons is being horsed from Prince Rock to Lee Moor, or from Lee Moor to Prince Rock, the Signalman at Mount Gould Junction Box, must, before giving the Driver permission to cross the Yealmpton Branch line, draw over No. 12 lever to the forward position. This will have the effect of locking all the points and signals leading to or from the Yealmpton Branch line, and at the same time the lever is itself automatically locked, and closes the four Throw-off points before referred to, so that the Tramway may be continuous for the Tram Wagons to pass.

As soon as one of the wheel tyres of the first Tram Wagon, and of the succeeding ones, touches the flat iron bar referred to, the bar will be depressed, and will cause the electric circuit to be broken in the first of the contact boxes referred to.

As the Tram Wagons proceed over each succeeding Section of the iron bar arrangement, the contact becomes broken in like manner in the contact box relating to each of the several sections.

Breaking contact in this way causes the electric lock in the Signal Cabin to remain locking No. 12 lever to the forward position until the rear Tram Wagon has passed over the last flat bar of the series, and is clear of the Junction, when the Signalman must place his foot on the foot plunger, which will release the electric lock, and cause "Lock-off" to appear on the electric lock indicator. He can then move No. 12 lever to the back of the frame, thereby placing the four Throw-off points in the Tramway line to the open position, and unlocking the signals and points relating to the Yealmpton Branch. The Signalman must not move No. 12 lever from the forward position until he sees "Lock-off" on the indicator.

The primary object of the apparatus described is that so long as a wheel tyre of any Tram Wagon is touching either of the fouling bars referred to, and consequently fouling the Branch line, the Signalman is prevented from working the signals or the points for a train to pass to or from the Yealmpton Branch.

9. The emergency lever referred to in Clause 4, is provided in case any of the appliances should fail, and so interrupt the working of the Branch.

This, however, is a rare contingency, but if it should happen, the Signalman must unlock the padlock, place the lever in the vertical position, and padlock it there. He must also, at once, advise the Lineman.

This will switch out the electric lock, and the Signalman will have to work without the security of the Safety Apparatus.

He must then take particular care in working the trains of Tram Wagons to satisfy himself by observation that the Yealmpton Branch line is clear of obstruction before allowing any train to or from Yealmpton to approach the Junction.

When at any time the Signalman finds the electric locking apparatus defective, he must, if it be broad daylight, at once satisfy himself by observation from the Signal Box that there is no obstruction on the Yealmpton Branch line as would arise from a Tram Wagon having been accidentally left, fouling the line.

If it be not broad daylight, or the atmospheric conditions prevent a clear view from the Signal Box of the two sets of Throw-off points in the Tramway, he must at once leave his Box and walk to the place referred to and not return until he has satisfied himself by inspection that there is no obstruction.

Under no circumstances must the "Emergency lever" be brought into use until the Signalman first personally satisfies himself that the line at the Junction with the Yealmpton Branch is clear.

LEE MOOR LEVEL CROSSING.
Situate between Marsh Mills and Bickleigh Stations.

1. A Gateman will be on duty at this crossing (week days only) from the passing of the first until the passing of the last train of Tram Wagons. He may be absent for meals in accordance with his duty paper.

2. An electric indicator and bell are fixed at Lee Moor Level Crossing Signal Box, to shew when a train has left Bickleigh or Marsh Mills, as the case may be.

3. After the indicator shews "Up train on line," or "Down train on line," no Tram wagons or vehicles of any kind, nor any animals, must, under any circumstances, be allowed to pass over or foul the line of railway until after such train has passed.

4. Before Tram Wagons, or horses, are allowed to pass over, or foul the railway at Lee Moor, the Up and Down Signals worked from Lee Moor Level Crossing must be placed at "Danger," and be so kept until the line is again clear.

5. Before the Gateman at the crossing leaves duty, the crossing gates must be locked across the Tramway, and all signals be put to show "All right." The Signal Box must be locked up, and the key of it kept in the custody of the level crossing Gateman.

THE LEE MOOR TRAMWAY PRESERVATION SOCIETY

The study of railways has always been a source of great interest and pleasure to many people, in all walks of life, and for almost 50 years the Plymouth Railway Circle has enabled railway enthusiasts living in the City and the surrounding area to meet and share their mutual interest together.

Being a privately-owned mineral railway which actually ran through a part of Plymouth itself, the Lee Moor Tramway was well known to members of the Circle and, after the decision in 1960 by its owners, English Clays Lovering Pochin and Company, to abandon the tramway, feelings of concern arose for the future of the two locomotives that, by then, had already been out of use for some 15 years. It was felt that efforts should be made to save at least one of them from possible sale to a scrap merchant, and eventually an approach was made to the owners with this end in view. The result was a very favourable reaction from the Clay Company, and it was suggested that a lease of the locomotive shed at Torycombe, together with both of the engines, be drawn up. This would then enable the work of restoration to commence, and a museum to be formed that centred around the line. A difficulty arose, however, in that the rules of the Plymouth Railway Circle contained no provision for actual preservation. As a result, it became necessary to form a separate organisation, the 'Lee Moor Tramway Preservation Society', which came into being early in 1964 with many, but not all, members coming from within the Circle. The Clay Company, meanwhile, was very helpful to the Society, as indeed it was to be on many subsequent occasions, and the lease was granted at a nominal rent of £1 per annum.

Initial inspection of the shed revealed that it had been subject to flooding and that the smoke ventilators in the roof had rusted badly, allowing rain to reach the bodywork of the engines, particularly 'LEE MOOR No 1'. It was also discovered that the inspection pit beneath the locomotives was partly filled with china clay slurry, and that at the sides of the shed were benches on which lay a variety of tools and spares. As for the siting of the locomotives, 'LEE MOOR No 1' was at the far (western) end of the shed, with her motion partially dismantled, whilst 'LEE MOOR No 2', being the last in use, had been run in behind her when services ceased. Both faced towards Cann Wood.

Society working parties, held on Wednesday evenings and some Saturday afternoons, commenced in May 1964, the first tasks being to form a soakaway around the shed to alleviate the flooding, the cleaning out of the inspection pit and the wiring of the building so that electric light and power could be provided by the Clay Company from its main supply. Wooden-framed shutters covered with metal sheeting were also made and fitted to the windows, whilst the owners carried out work to remove the roof ventilators and to make the building weatherproof. A short length of track was also relaid outside the shed so as to enable the engines to be moved into the open when necessary. As 'No 2' was nearer the door, it was decided that her restoration should be the first priority, whilst 'No 1' was left to await her turn – although not before being 'painted' with old engine oil in an effort to prevent further corrosion! At that time it was not even certain that the restoration of the second locomotive could be carried out, but it was always felt that it should be done if the Society membership was prepared to undertake the work. What was certain, however, was the fact that the locomotives were never likely to progress beyond becoming static exhibits, for the Society had neither the equipment nor experience to restore them to working order, added to which the unusual gauge meant that new track would have to be laid on which they could be operated, and that was clearly an impossibility.

Having completed the necessary preliminary work in and around the shed, the working parties were soon able to set about restoring 'No 2'. Initially, this involved removing external piping, fittings and motion, followed by the burning off of the paintwork in order to expose the metal surfaces; these were then cleaned with wire brushes before being treated with a rust preventative. The next stage was to fill the portions of the top of the saddle tank and the front of the smokebox, which had been badly pitted by years of rain entering through the derelict roof ventilators. Progress was not rapid, as working parties met usually only once a week but, nevertheless, by the end of the first season a considerable amount had already been achieved. Doubtless, even more progress would have been made in the winter evenings for there was certainly adequate lighting in the shed. However, the damp moorland air caused considerable condensation on the metal surfaces of the locomotive, thus making rust proofing or painting impracticable.

Work resumed in the summer of 1965, and again in 1966, by which time the cleaning down of 'No 2' above the footplate had been largely completed, and she had received a coat of yellow chromate paint. Indeed, on 18th May 1966 a notable event occurred in that 'No 2' was pushed out of the shed onto the relaid length of track – the first time she had been in the open air for over 20 years! The members of the working party were so elated by their achievement that they also managed to move a very reluctant 'No 1' outside the shed to join her sister. Needless to say, apart from clicking camera shutters, there was not a lot more work done that evening!

The summer of 1967 saw steady progress continuing, and by the end of the working season the upper part of the locomotive had received its top coat of green paint. Much of the yellow and black lining had also been completed. In addition, it was discovered that the remains of one of the tramway's wagons was lying in Cann Wood, having apparently run away on the incline sometime in the 1930s. As all the other wagons had, of course, been scrapped, this was a fortunate discovery, and plans were made, with the full co-operation of the Clay Company, for its recovery and eventual rebuilding.

Although the restoration of a locomotive, and now a wagon, was the principal aim of the Society, other relics of the tramway were being displayed inside the shed. These included one of the signals that had previously guarded the level-crossing with the GWR main line at Laira, together with items of

The two Lee Moor Tramway locomotives photographed outside the Torycombe shed on 18th May 1966 – the first time that they had been in the open air for over 20 years!

general interest from railways in the district, and train headboards from enthusiasts' railtours.

During the following year (1968) the Clay Company again gave great support to the Society in two ways; firstly by constructing replacement wooden tool-boxes for the engine at their carpenters' shop at Lee Moor and, secondly, by retrieving the remains of the wagon and delivering them to the shed on the 17th July, along with four springs which had been unearthed from the blacksmiths' shop. Unfortunately, the woodwork of the wagon was found to be beyond repair, but such was the level of enthusiasm that the construction of a new body commenced, the work being carried out mainly by a single Society member working in his garage! Later, parts of a long-dismantled wagon were discovered

Partially restored 'LEE MOOR No 2' seen outside the shed at Torycombe on 25th February 1968.

and brought down from the site of the stone siding near the top of the Torycombe incline. These were then subsequently added to the parts from the Cann Wood wagon to complete the necessary ironwork.

Meanwhile, progress on 'No 2' centred mainly on the frames, cylinders and motion, jobs that involved working in cramped conditions in the inspection pit below the engine. Also, in the early part of the 1969 working season, the sections of completed woodwork which were to form the body of the rebuilt wagon were brought to the shed in order that reconstruction could commence. A problem then presented itself in that the shed was not long enough to accommodate two locomotives and a wagon. The solution, however, was to remove the buffers from 'No 1' and move her as far into the shed as possible, thereby creating just sufficient additional space for the wagon.

Members of the L.M.T.P.S. giving the chassis of the restored wagon a trial outing on 18th June 1969. The Chairman of the Society, Chris Soper, is on the left of the picture, with his wife seated on the wagon.

By the end of the year the wagon had been reassembled and the painting and lining-out of 'No 2' had been completed, leaving only the finishing touches to be added in the following summer of 1970. During this period, when the restoration of the locomotive and wagon was approaching completion, details were circulated concerning a proposed Steam Traction Rally which was to be held in Chelson Meadow, near Saltram House, in July 1970. Although primarily intended for steam road vehicles, the Society felt that this could be an ideal opportunity to display the result of their labours to the public. So, with the full agreement of the Clay Company, who promised to provide transport on a low loader at no cost to the Society, it was resolved to take the locomotive and wagon to the rally.

During discussions amongst Society members whilst working on the locomotive, it was realised that there existed a situation in North Wales which was similar in many respects to that at Lee Moor. In the former case, Lord Penrhyn owned slate quarries at Bethesda, which were connected to the coast by a private mineral railway. The family home was Penrhyn Castle, which was now in the care of the National Trust, and it contained a museum that included locomotives and other exhibits from the railway. In the case of the Lee Moor Tramway, the landowner was the Earl of Morley, whose home at Saltram House was also in the care of the National Trust. Moreover, it was only a short distance from Chelson Meadow, and quickly gave rise to the feeling that if a similar museum could be formed at Saltram, it would provide an ideal home for the engine and wagon – away from the damp conditions of the shed at Torycombe.

The idea was then put to the Clay Company (which, of course, was still the legal owner of the locomotive) and it willingly agreed to make a joint approach to the National Trust regarding the formation of such a museum. The outcome was an offer from the Trust to house the exhibits in the vacant Coach House at Saltram, and this was accepted as being an ideal situation in which the locomotive and wagon could be viewed by the public for many years to come. An additional, and very great, advantage was that the museum building could be occupied immediately after the Steam Traction Rally at Chelson Meadow, thus obviating the need to return to the shed at Torycombe.

The restoration of 'No 2' and the wagon was finally completed by the middle of July 1970, and on the 17th of that month they were transported on a low loader to the rally at Chelson Meadow. Here, they remained on view until being taken on to Saltram House on 20th July. The transfer from the low loader to the Coach House that followed, however, proved to be a difficult operation, involving not only a lift by crane over a fence but also a push by many willing volunteers across a cobbled yard into the building; this was relatively simple in the case of the truck, but much more effort was required to move the locomotive, which necessitated the use of steel plates. Nevertheless, by late evening, and much to the satisfaction of the members of the Preservation Society, the move had been completed.

A little over a week later, on 29th July 1970, the work of restoring 'LEE MOOR No 1' commenced. Here, the same procedure was followed to that of the first restoration, but with the benefit of experience and also with much more space being available in the Torycombe shed, progress was such that the job was completed by 20th November 1974. By then, the Clay Company and the Preservation Society had already reached an agreement concerning the future of 'No 1' whereby, on completion, it would be taken to Wheal Martyn, near St. Austell, where a museum covering the history of the china clay industry was in the process of being founded. Consequently, arrangements were put in hand for the necessary transportation, and the journey to Cornwall was eventually made on 17th March 1975. This, in fact, was a few days before the official opening of the museum on 26th March 1975, a ceremony which

'LEE MOOR No 2' and wagon seen outside the locomotive shed at Torycombe in July 1970, restoration work now having been completed.

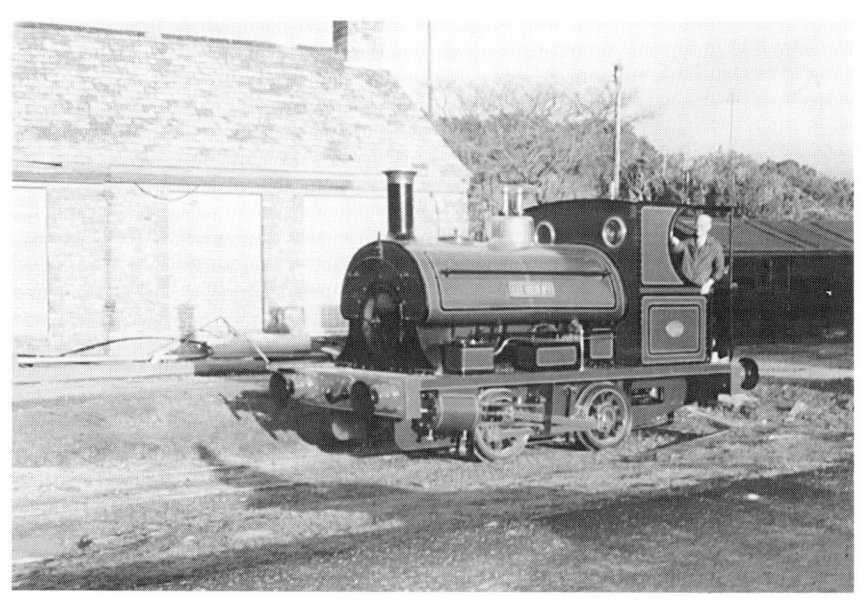

'LEE MOOR No 1' photographed at Torycombe, after restoration, on 23rd November 1974.

A head-on view of 'LEE MOOR No 1', taken on the same date as the photograph above.

'LEE MOOR No 1' being lowered onto the road transporter at Torycombe on 17th March 1975.

was attended by several members of the Society at the invitation of the Clay Company and one that provided a fitting conclusion to the original aims of the preservationists. Thus, after a period of three quarters of a century, the locomotive shed at Torycombe stood empty, and it remained only to dismantle and remove the smaller exhibits, which were subsequently either taken to the museums or returned to their individual owners.

As a postscript to the story of the locomotives, it is worth recording that one of the original works plates from 'LEE MOOR No 2' has been displayed in a showcase at the National Railway Museum at York. It would appear to have been donated to the Museum when the tramway became disused, as it was missing from the locomotive when the Preservation Society first entered the Torycombe shed. However, a new plate was cast and affixed to the engine during its restoration.

It needs also to be mentioned that as a token of appreciation of the work carried out on the locomotives, the Clay Company donated 'LEE MOOR No 2' to the Plymouth Railway Circle (into which the Preservation Society had reverted when the completion of its aims drew near) and that the engine remains under the care of the Circle in the Coach House at Saltram.

Membership Card

LEE MOOR TRAMWAY PRESERVATION SOCIETY

This is to certify the membership of:

Miss A. Shepherd

Number 72

Ivor R. Hocking
Hon. Secretary

Valid only as over.

Two photographs taken in the museum at Saltram House on 9th September 1996. *Above:* 'LEE MOOR No 2'. *Below:* The restored wagon (numbered 44).

THE REMAINS OF THE ROUTES IN 1996

The exploration of a railway system which, as previously stated, has been abandoned in stages from 1847 to 1960 will reveal that some portions can be found with comparative ease, whilst others have disappeared without trace. It depends very much on the geographical locations rather than the dates of abandonment and, certainly so far as the main route of the Plymouth & Dartmoor Railway is concerned, results in the middle and upper sections being readily apparent in many places, whereas the lower section in and around Plymouth has been almost completely obliterated.

Before undertaking an exploration of any part of the remains of the routes, it is worth mentioning that the whole of the area through which the railways ran is covered by the following Ordnance Survey maps, to a scale of 1:25,000 ($2^{1}/_{2}$ inches to 1 mile):–

(i) Outdoor Leisure Map No 28 'Dartmoor'
(ii) Pathfinder Map No 1356 'Plymouth'

It also needs to be mentioned that old quarries are places of considerable danger, so please take care. Remember, too, that some parts of the various routes are now on private land and should not be entered without first seeking permission from the owner(s) concerned.

(a) THE PLYMOUTH & DARTMOOR RAILWAY:–

1. Sutton Harbour, Plymouth to Leigham Tunnel.

The most logical place to begin an exploration would, ordinarily, be at the site of the southern terminus, at a wharf known as Johnson's Quay (SX 488542) on the eastern side of Sutton Harbour. However, not only has the site been cleared but the portion of the harbour by the quay has been filled in as part of a scheme that included the installation of a sea-lock at the harbour entrance. As a result, all traces of the railway here have been lost.

From the quay, the line ran eastwards across Sutton Road (at its junction with Commercial Road) and continued along the northern side of the modern Barbican Approach to enter a shallow cutting – now used as a one-way relief road named Gdynia Way. After leaving this cutting and passing under a pedestrian bridge, it then crossed Laira Bridge Road and entered the area currently occupied by the Western National Omnibus garage (SX 498545). This, in fact, was where the triangular junction with the branch to Martin's Wharf, on the Cattewater, which also formed part of the Lee Moor Tramway, formerly existed.

Martin's Wharf can be viewed from the pavement on the southern side of the A379 road bridge over the Plym estuary (SX 501542) but, here again, all traces of the railway have been lost: the wharf has been rebuilt (it is now used as a yacht park) and all the old buildings have been demolished. However, the bridge under the A379, which was shared with the L&SWR

Cattewater branch, is still used by a standard-gauge railway line at the time of writing, the only noticeable change being an extension built onto its southern side. Beyond the bridge, on its northern side, the route is lost in an area of industrial buildings, but it ran behind the Western National Omnibus garage. Here, part of it is currently used as a parking area for buses and coaches, and can be seen from the pedestrian footbridge near the end of Embankment Lane (SX 499546).

A photograph of the bridge by which the line passed under Embankment Road prior to being filled in. To the right can be seen the rails of the GWR Sutton Harbour line.

The bridge, by which the line passed under Embankment Road, has been filled in, but the formation curves around on waste ground at the rear of Stanley Place. The line then proceeded under the embankment of the Cattewater branch by means of a further bridge, which has also been filled in, and ran along the western side of a pre-cast concrete works. Previously, this was the point to which the last 'right of way' sand trains were operated.

On either side of Lanhydrock Road bridge a carriage washing plant adjoins the route of the old line, which then reached the side of the former level-crossing with the Yealmpton branch. After running behind a row of houses at Arnold's Point, it subsequently curved to run between the present BR High-Speed Train sidings and Embankment Road before reaching the main BR line at Laira level-crossing. Since the tramway's closure, the BR line has been re-ballasted to a higher level, but the site of the crossing is, coincidently, marked by milepost 244.

Two views, looking towards Crabtree, of the remains of the embankment that carried the line up to the northern side of the Forder Valley. Note the stone sleeper blocks scattered down the side of the embankment, which was completely removed in 1993.

From this point the next section of the route is completely lost under modern road improvements, but it ran approximately along the line of the footpath on the southern side of the A374 Plymouth Road, passing the small tidal creek where was sited the original terminus of the railway. The junction with the Lee Moor Tramway was close to where stands The Marsh Mill Travel Inn, and from here the line ran across the main A38 and on past the present-day buildings of a large car sales and service premises to reach the start of the long embankment that carried it up to the northern side of the valley. The embankment, though, has been completely removed, and the hillside excavated to form a site for the large, modern retail stores now there. Beyond this, on the southern side of Longbridge Road, office blocks and a hotel have been erected on the route, which then crossed what is currently known as Wilburt Road near its junction with Barnstaple Close.

At the junction of Wilburt Road and Forder Valley Road, a narrow path leads up to the formation of the railway, which, hereabouts, is now used as a public footpath. This, in turn, follows the side of the valley along the Forder Valley Local Nature Reserve and provides the opportunity to see some of the stone sleeper blocks that still remain. Milestone 3 stands on the western side of the line at SX 508579, and the path continues to within a short distance of the southern portal of Leigham Tunnel. Unfortunately, the route is then overgrown and becomes impassable as it enters the cutting leading to the tunnel, but the portal, which is sealed with a heavy steel barrier, can be viewed from the field on the southern side.

In order to rejoin the route it is necessary to cross Sheepstor and Brampton Roads before entering Plymbridge Road, which leads down to the northern portal of the tunnel at SX 514587. This, too, is sealed, and in similar fashion to that of its southern counterpart.

2. Leigham Tunnel to Roborough (Jump)

From the northern portal of the tunnel, the route (now part of the road) passes Tunnel Cottages before bearing away on the northern side and becoming a public footpath that follows the contours of the valley. There are many

stone sleeper blocks hereabouts and milestone 4 soon comes into view on the eastern side (SX 519587). Some distance farther on, and approaching the public road from Plym Bridge to Roborough, a private road to a housing estate is crossed on the level followed by a wooden footbridge over the public road; this is built on the abutments of the former railway bridge. The path then continues along the hillside and, as Rumple Quarry is neared, it is clear that part of the track-bed has, at some time in the past, collapsed down the steep slope. Doubtless, this is the 'landslip' referred to by the writer of an article on the railway in the December 1908 issue of the *Railway Magazine*.

After passing the workings of Rumple Quarry, the site of the fifth milestone is reached at SX 521599; this used to stand on the eastern side of the route, but

Stone sleeper blocks on the route in the Plym Valley, a short distance above milestone 4.

The course of the railway curving towards Common Wood, in the Plym Valley.

disappeared sometime between 1957 and 1964. The path, meanwhile, can be followed to the point where a gate across the route (SX 520601) marks the termination of public access. It is then possible to pass through a field on the eastern side of the route and to rejoin it at the other end, but after only a very short distance another area of private land is encountered.

Above Common Wood lies the section of track where the line doubled back on itself several times in order to traverse small side valleys. Here, it also passed the site of milestone 6 before running through what is now an area of residential caravans at Glen Holt, the railway's hillside formation having been widened to accommodate the dwellings some 30 years ago. This, of course, is again private land, and the route only becomes accessible once more as the head of a side valley is crossed at SX 508606 prior to continuing along the wooded hillside past the site of the now-vanished milestone 7.

This latter portion of the line can be best approached by the pathway (signposted 'To Bickleigh Vale') leading over a stone stile adjoining a gate on the eastern side of the A386, near the entrance to the Woolwell roundabout (SX 501613). The pathway crosses the formation at SX 505611, and from this point the track-bed can be traced back to the caravan park as well as in the opposite direction, through more woodland, towards Darklake Farm. There is a second point of access through a gate at the end of Maple Way (SX 511610) on the Woolwell estate, but beyond this point the next part of the route cannot be followed as it is completely overgrown until it passes milestone 8 (on the western side at SX 513612) and runs over a high embankment leading to the gate to Darklake Farm.

From Darklake Farm the route, now used as an access to fields, runs through farmland and passes the site of milestone 9, but cannot be seen again until it reaches a public road at Blackeven Hill (SX 510624). Here, on the western side of the road, a hedge has now been erected across the formation, but previously it was possible to see a roughly shaped rectangular stone at this location. Measuring 2 ft. 3 in. by 1 ft. 4 in., with a depth of 7 in. and a groove 5½ in. wide and 2½ in. deep on its upper surface, the stone was possibly one of a number laid across the road to recess the rails at the level-crossing.

Beyond the road, the next part of the route has been absorbed by fields, reappearing only as it crosses a lane at SX 506624. From this point it is then used as a private approach to dwellings, prior to emerging on the western side of Roborough Village Recreation Hall at SX 504625.

The grooved stone that was possibly one of a number laid across the road to recess the rails for the level-crossing at Blackeven Hill.

3. Roborough (Jump) to Yennadon Cross.

From the Recreation Hall, the line crossed New Road and ran on the eastern side of the A386 towards Yelverton for about 300 yards. It then curved north-eastwards to follow field hedges through the private lands of Leigh Farm, where milestone 10 stands at SX 506630. Beyond the farm, the route turns northwards to where it may be seen again making an oblique crossing of Little Down Lane at SX 511633. It then re-enters private ground for a short distance, passing at the rear of some dwellings, but can be rejoined by continuing along Little Down Lane to just north of the cattle grid at SX 510636.

Here, a rough road leads downhill on the eastern side, with sleeper blocks placed along its verge. After a short distance, the course of the railway emerges from the south through a metal gate, and continues across this road to the southern extremity of Roborough Down. From this point the route takes a winding course across the open Down until it reaches a level-crossing over the road to Clearbrook at SX 517650. This portion of the line is, however, difficult to trace, being mostly heavily overgrown with gorse and bracken, but milestone 11 can be found beside a tree (SX 510642), and a single bridge carries the track-bed over the Plymouth Leat and across Roborough Down Lane on the level at SX 515647.

On the northern side of the road to Clearbrook a shallow, curving cutting leads towards the Wharf building (SX 517651). This is now used by the nearby golf club and is of interest in that an opening in the centre section of both end-walls has been filled with stonework; it seems probable that a siding ran into, or through, the structure at some time. Incidentally, it was formerly possible to see stone rails (as distinct from sleeper blocks)

forming a siding on the western side of the curved cutting, but these have now become overgrown by turf.

Northwards from this point the formation is less overgrown, and can mostly be followed without undue difficulty past milestone 12 (SX 516653), with sleeper blocks visible in places. After a short distance a modern stone stile leads into a section between stone walls, at the northern end of which a gate gives access to open Down once again. The course then becomes a rough road serving houses on its eastern side, whilst the dry channels of the Plymouth and Devonport leats close in to run beside the route of the railway on either side.

After some distance, milestone 13 (SX 520667) is passed on the western side and the course becomes covered by tarmac, which continues until the road bends sharply to the west. Here, the stone sleeper blocks reappear ahead, with a single length of rail remaining in situ at SX 517672. In addition, the Devonport Leat is crossed a short distance farther on by a narrow footbridge; this is obviously not original, although the stone abutments supporting it almost certainly are.

Stone sleeper blocks and the single remaining rail near Yelverton.

Beyond this bridge, however, the route becomes overgrown on the approach to the main A386 and is lost as it traverses the area of the wartime Harrowbeer airfield. It, nevertheless, ran eastwards at this point to recross the road near the present Yelverton roundabout, where stone sleeper blocks appear again for a short distance – between the road leading towards the Methodist Church and a row of buildings and shops at the entrance to Eastella Road. This, in fact, was where the B3212 was crossed diagonally on the level, but no visible signs of the crossing remain or, indeed, of the nearby stone-railed siding which ran to a walled wharf at, or near, the present petrol filling station. Interestingly enough, the stones have been relaid to form the edging of the roundabout.

From the entrance to Eastella Road the route is again lost, but it continued in an easterly direction through the area of modern private dwellings to a point a little north of the junction of Kirkella and Midella Roads. Here, at SX 526679, it was joined by the track-bed of the later, standard-gauge railway to Princetown, which approached this location through a deep cutting; this has now been filled in and built over, but the parapets of a bridge that formerly crossed the line can be seen from Southella Road.

Onwards towards the moor, the combined route of the two railways is inaccessible as it passes through fields and crosses a bridge over the lane to Lake. It is, however, visible again as it comes up to run along the southern side of the Princetown road (SX 531686) before reaching Dousland and the former GWR station. At Dousland, of course, there has been considerable housing development, but the route ran from the station area through what is now Stowford Close and Barons Road estate before crossing the road to Sheepstor by means of a level-crossing. Then, on the opposite side of the road, where further new housing covers the site of the track-bed, it ran between Manor Park and the Sheepstor road, crossed Iron Mine Lane at a spot now occupied by a dwelling aptly named 'The Crossing' and, finally, reached the open moorland of Yennadon Down at SX 542679, where it is possible, once more, to gain access to the joint formation of the two railways.

Looking back towards Dousland from here, the route can be seen running between low stone walls, whilst in the opposite direction it leads out onto the Down. And it is now, after a very short distance, that the remarkable horseshoe bend commences by which the earlier railway turned in a complete half-circle in order to gain height. The formation, itself, is overgrown with gorse bushes, but can be followed as it diverges on a low embankment from the later line and then curves sharply to cross it prior to entering a shallow cutting. (This feature is shown very clearly on the 1:25,000 Dartmoor Outdoor Leisure Map). Beyond the (sometimes wet) cutting, the route soon reaches a locked field gate, with a pedestrian access on one side, and is subsequently swallowed up by a surfaced road that continues to the top of Iron Mine Lane. The route then re-emerges to cross the lane for a second time, after which it enters the private drive of a dwelling. However, a rough road can be followed around the curtilage, and this later rejoins the route on its northern side.

Two photographs depicting the acute bend of the railway as it reaches Yennadon Down. The upper shows the sharply curved embankment looking towards Dousland, whilst the lower (taken from the right-hand side of the view in the other photograph) shows the route heading towards Princetown through a gorse-lined cutting after crossing the formation of the later, standard-gauge railway to Princetown.

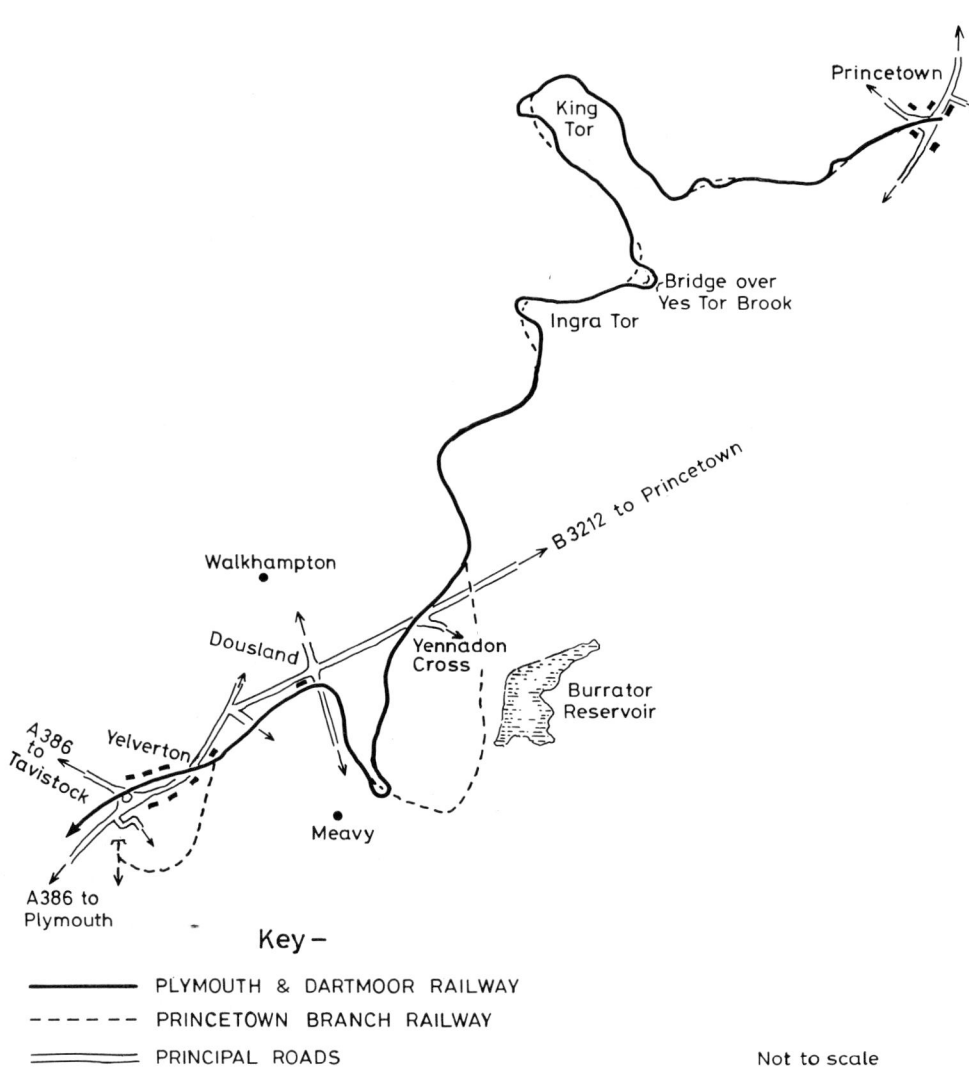

The road is used by lorries going to and from a quarry, but beyond this it reverts to a track which shortly passes through a gate into private land (SX 542690). Meanwhile, after running through a field, a belt of trees and the grounds of a private house, the route of the railway finally emerges again to cross the B3212 at Yennadon Cross (SX 545694).

4. Yennadon Cross to the Quarries and Princetown.

From the site of the level-crossing over the B3212, the route runs through an open space now used as a road lay-by and is then absorbed by fields. Nevertheless, part of the course can be identified as it follows a stone wall and crosses the lane leading to Peekhill Farm, where the approach embankments of the former bridge remain. This part of the old line is on private land, but it can be viewed from the B3212, and it is possible to follow a 'Permitted Path' along the formation of the Princetown railway. This leads from a stile at the bottom of Peek Hill (SX 549696), where the later line has also been absorbed by fields, until rejoining the earlier line to the east of Horseyeatt Farm. The actual point of junction, however, can no longer be precisely identified.

The greater part of the remainder of the route to Princetown was taken over by the later railway, and stone sleeper blocks can be seen in, or beside, the formation in many places. A careful examination will also show that some have been incorporated into the stonework of several underbridges, which were built to carry the standard-gauge line. In the meantime, once the last of a number of gates and stiles have been negotiated, access is gained to the open moor of Walkhampton Common, where, after about a mile, a diversion from the later line can be found on the eastern side at SX 554720. A flat area here may also have been the site of sidings but, whatever, the older formation initially runs parallel to the route of the Princetown railway. It then passes across the later line before rounding a considerable curve (SX 553721) and returning to the combined route as the entrance to the quarry at Ingra Tor is passed on the southern side.

Continuing towards Princetown, an accommodation overbridge spans a shallow cutting and, after a short distance, as the Princetown railway curves to the north over a high embankment, the older route turns eastwards. Here, it runs in a semi-circle and crosses the Yes Tor Brook by means of a masonry bridge (SX 565725), the structure of which is still in generally good condition. Admittedly, the upstream side has been eroded by the stream, but the downstream stonework remains much as it must have appeared when first constructed over 170 years ago. Some remedial work that has recently been carried out at either end of the bridge (which is considerably wider than seems necessary to carry a single line of rails) has also helped. Meanwhile, beyond the bridge, the formation runs between stone walls before crossing the Princetown railway at a slightly higher level and turning to the north to rejoin it at SX 564728, near the ruins of Yes Tor Farm.

The route of the railway curving around the valley of the Yes Tor Brook. The bridge over the stream lies hidden behind the large rock in the foreground, whilst the route of the later, standard-gauge railway to Princetown, which crosses the valley on the dark embankment seen towards the left of the picture, cuts through the earlier route in the centre. Above this latter point, on the hillside, can be seen the inclined plane between two waste stone tips.

The upstream portal of the bridge over the Yes Tor Brook, showing the erosion caused by the stream.

Disregarding the lines to the quarries, which are described in the next chapter, traces of the old line are next seen at SX 555737. At this point the track-bed can be seen running to the east of the derelict buffer stop that marks the end of the Princetown railway siding leading back to the Swelltor quarries. It then goes past the remains of a stone loading bank standing beside the route a short distance before it is crossed by the later line and proceeds around a quite spectacular bend. The track of the Princetown railway, meanwhile, goes through a cutting with a less acute curve, and it is just beyond here that the two routes merge once more.

When the vicinity of the Foggintor quarry tips is reached many pieces of loose stone are scattered along and around the somewhat indistinct track-bed, but after crossing the rough track to Yes Tor Farm the course is clear once again. A short distance farther on the route of the Princetown railway rises on an embankment to cross a small valley (SX 571732), but the original route took a more northerly course, at first, and there are now remains of part of an embankment and bridge over a small stream in the vicinity. Then, on the southern side, a curve around the hillside took it outside the cutting of the later line, although apart from a few sleeper blocks, there is little to be seen. Thereafter, the only other spot where there might have been a (small) deviation is on the northern side of the route at SX 582733, near the head of the River Meavy. This, however, is by no means certain, nor are any remains visible at the location.

91

The routes of the two railways rounding the bend below King's Tor. The earlier route curves to the left of the picture, whilst that of the later, standard-gauge railway to Princetown first crosses it and then passes through a cutting to the right.

A photograph taken near Foggintor showing, from left to right, the broad formation of the combined route of the two railways, the shallow cutting where was situated the GWR's Royal Oak siding and the now rush-grown route of the P. & D.R. branch to the nearby quarries. In the centre of the picture is the former site of King Tor Halt (GWR), and here the route was crossed by the rough road to Yes Tor Farm.

As the track-bed approaches Princetown, the site of the former GWR station, through which the Plymouth & Dartmoor Railway ran, is seen ahead; the buildings have been demolished and the site has been fenced off. A path, however, follows the southern perimeter of the site and, after passing a building formerly used as a stable (but not by the earlier railway), the route can be regained once again: it forms the approach road to the former GWR station, leading past the Fire Station and a car park on the right-hand side. The final few yards have been obliterated, but the line curved so as to pass in front of the Duchy Hotel (now The High Moorland Visitor Centre) and to cross the Two Bridges to Yelverton road. The railway then terminated at a depot situated at The Railway Inn.

The railway to Marsh Mills.

The railway to Marsh Mills has been almost completely obliterated by road building and other development, but the junction of this line and the railway to Princetown was sited near what is now The Marsh Mill Travel Inn (SX 516566). From there, the route ran through the present roundabout and flyover area to reach the Longbridge Road. Then comes the one remaining feature of the line, the bridge over the River Plym (SX 520568), which is now used as a footpath and retains rails, although a low flood prevention wall has been erected across them on either side of the river.

The bridge over the River Plym, and Weighbridge Cottage. Although this photograph was taken in the 1920s, the scene remains essentially unchanged.
F. H. C. Casbourn, courtesy of The Stephenson Locomotive Society

The remainder of the course can only be imagined as it passed through the site currently occupied by two large retail stores, and crossed the site of Marsh Mills GWR station. On the eastern side of the station the final section leading to the terminal basin of the Cann Quarry canal ran northwards through the area now occupied by a third large retail shop and its car park (SX 522568).

The railway to Cann Quarry.

This part of the system branched from the Marsh Mills route at Weighbridge Cottage (SX 520568) and can be followed as a footpath towards the road leading to the former War Department depot at Coypool. The railway ran immediately to the east of the path, and here some rails remain, laid with chaired track, but almost completely covered by undergrowth and bushes. At the end of the footpath, the route curved to the north across the road, ran past the present site of the Plym Valley Railway and entered what is now the Plym Valley Cycle Path, which is also used as a footpath.

A short distance along this path, a wartime standard-gauge line serving the Coypool depot crossed the earlier line on the level; this has also now been dismantled.

The Cycle Path has been formed on the course of the railway as far as Plym Bridge, and occasional slatestone sleepers may be seen lying alongside the way. The former level-crossing with the GWR branch to Tavistock and Launceston is located at SX 519581, and some distance farther on, at SX 521584, a tree-grown embankment is visible on the western side of the trackbed of the GWR branch. This is of interest as being a section of the original route which had to be abandoned when the line to Tavistock was built through the valley.

A short distance farther on, the Lee Moor Tramway diverged at SX 522585, whilst the Cann Quarry line reached the road at Plym Bridge. Access to the continuation of the route is gained through a gate on the other side of the road: after passing under the GWR by means of a bridge shared with the Cann Quarry canal, the remainder of the course to the quarry forms a very pleasant wooded walk beside the canal, with stone sleepers remaining in situ in places. Approaching the quarry, the course runs on a narrow shelf between the river and the embankment of the GWR Cann viaduct, before passing under the viaduct and into the quarry (SX 524596). The walls of some of the quarry buildings remain, but the site is overgrown and partially flooded, and should only be entered with great care.

A photograph taken near Plym Bridge showing where the line to Cann Quarry crossed the road on the level before passing underneath the (right-hand) bridge shared with the Cann Quarry canal.

The railway to Plympton.

The line to Plympton was the first part of the system to be closed, in 1847, so it is not surprising that almost 150 years later little remains to be seen.

The raised footpath at the side of the Plymouth Road which formed part of the course of the railway to Plympton.

Although running beside what is now a busy road, one feature that does survive is the raised footpath (part of the former course of the railway) between Larkham Lane (SX 529566) and Dingle Road (SX 533565). An elderly local resident, then aged 80, stated in 1960 that he remembered blue slatestone sleepers still remaining here.

The final section, crossing the former GWR main line and running to the depot building at SX 537565, which was demolished in 1981, has completely disappeared.

The terminus was sited at the rear of the existing row of shops at St. Mary's Bridge, in an area which later became the goods yard of the GWR station at Plympton. This, too, has now been built over, to form the housing development of St. Mary's Court and St. Mary's Close.

The short line to Farm Quarry diverged approximately between Great Woodford Drive and the Union Inn. The quarry, in private land, is overgrown and partially filled, whilst no trace of the tunnel can be seen.

b) THE LEE MOOR TRAMWAY:–

The route of the tramway extended from Martin's Wharf on the Cattewater to the Lee Moor area, but this, of course, included portions of the original Plymouth & Dartmoor, Marsh Mills and Cann Quarry Railways. To complete the survey, therefore, it is necessary only to consider the section from the junction with the Cann Quarry line near Plym Bridge (SX 522585) to Lee Moor.

From the site of the junction it is possible to walk to the foot of the Cann Wood incline, and here the ruins of the brick-built stables can be seen on the eastern side. Access to the incline, though, is barred by a derelict bridge over the canal, and by a fence. The other bridge, across the Plympton to Plym Bridge road, is not the original one, but a later replacement carrying the pipeline which superseded the tramway.

The next point of access is reached by turning off the Plympton to Shaugh Prior road into the Forestry Commission car park at SX 547597. From here, it is possible to walk along forestry tracks for about three quarters of a mile to reach the summit of the Cann Wood incline at SX 538594. The timber beams and decking of a bridge, by which the tramway crossed the forestry road, have been removed, and only the stone piers remain. On the western side, the course of the incline descends through trees, whilst the former winding drum-houses stand on the eastern side of the bridge, also in woodland. The drum-houses, which were built partly above ground level, have been filled with sand, and the area around them is fenced off to prevent access. Nothing remains of the shed which formerly stood across the tracks above the drum-houses.

Regaining the Shaugh Prior road, and turning north, the site of Whitegates level-crossing is reached at SX 546602. The original gates, signals and gatesman's hut have gone, and the route is protected by modern gates set back

The former tramway bridge over the road at Plym Bridge, at the lower end of the Cann Wood incline.

The stone engraved '1899' that up until a few years ago could still be seen in the remains of the wall on the western side of Whitegates level-crossing.

Truelove Bridge, where the course of the tramway can be seen passing through the cutting.

some distance from the road on either side. However, two of the tubular gate pillars still remain, along with part of a stone wall, on the western side. As late as 1984 a stone engraved '1899' could be seen in this wall, put there no doubt when the line was rebuilt to take the locomotives. It may still be there, but, if so, it is now covered by a thick growth of ivy.

A minor road nearby crosses Truelove Bridge (SX 549606), where the course of the tramway can be seen passing through the cutting. Beyond this point, the route soon approaches the extensive china clay workings, which are, of course, on private land with no public access. Nevertheless, the former locomotive shed can be viewed from the site of the level-crossing at Torycombe, standing on the western side of the road to Lee Moor (SX 565611). Stone walls have been built across the track-bed on each side of the public road, whilst the route of the tramway leading towards Cann Wood is now a private works road. The remainder of the course leading to its terminus in the Torycombe valley has been absorbed by the works area but the site of the second Torycombe incline may be viewed from the modern public road at SX 568615, which has been constructed across it a short distance below the summit.

The upper portion of the severed Torycombe (second) incline as seen from the adjoining road. Note the substantial construction of the embankment.

Stone sleepers on the course of the Wotter branch, looking towards Lee Moor.

In Lee Moor village the route crossed the road at SX 572620, and this is now the limit of public access. The track-bed, however, can be followed back across the area of grass in front of Blackalder, Saltram and Montague Terraces to a point where it becomes a works road. This, in turn, leads to the summit of the original, and later, Torycombe inclines and the commencement of the branch to Wotter, which is now almost entirely covered by sand spoil tips. The remainder of the formation of the tramway, from Lee Moor village to the terminus at Cholwichtown, is inaccessible, having been largely obliterated by spoil tips and other works.

In conclusion, it must be emphasised that much of the site of the tramway in the Torycombe and Lee Moor area is on land that is not accessible to the general public, and care should be taken in this respect at all times.

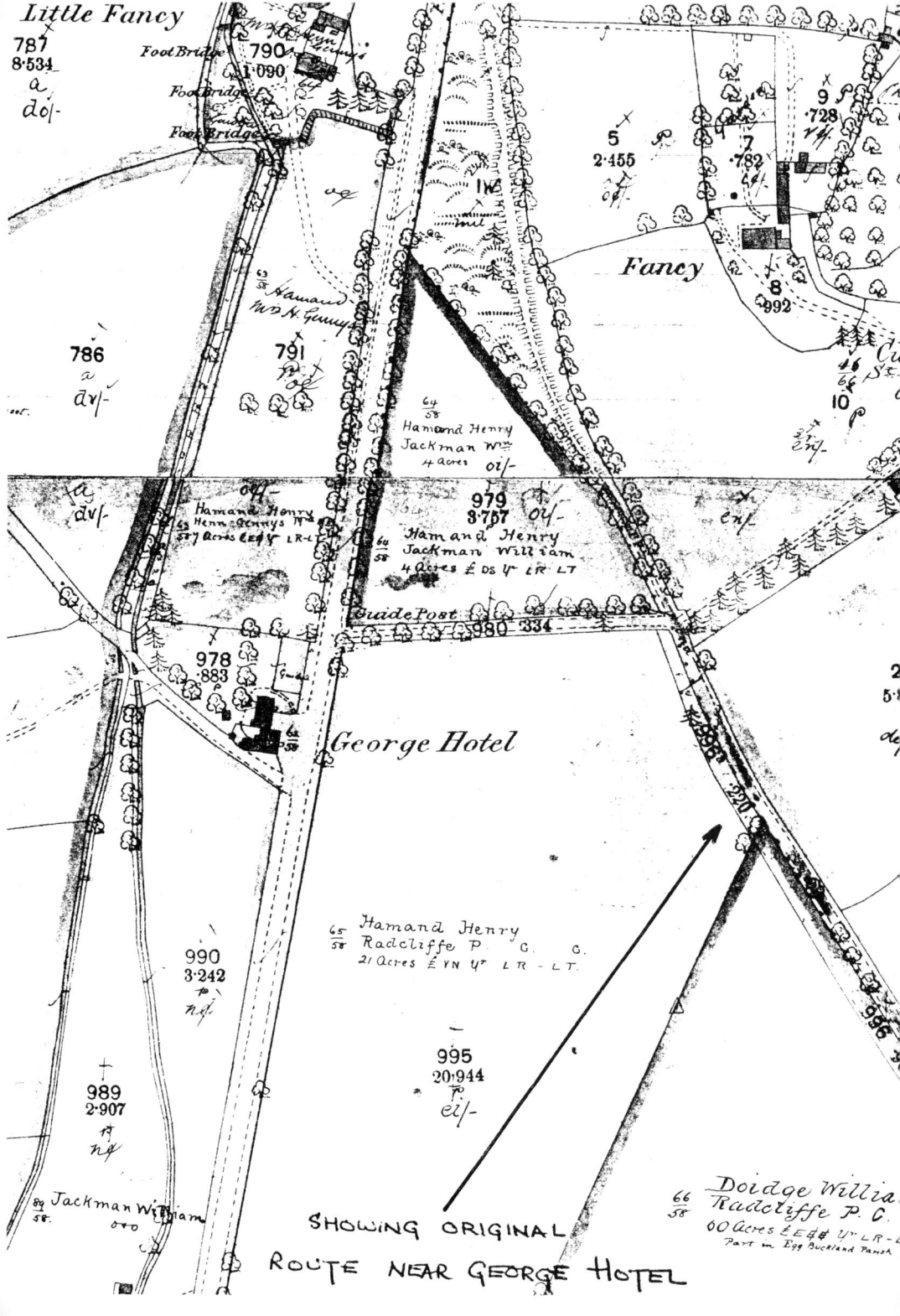

Having completed a description of the railways as they are at the time of writing, it is, perhaps, worth mentioning several matters which relate in various ways to the system. Firstly, there is near Roborough one portion of the originally-surveyed route of the Plymouth & Dartmoor line via Fursdon which is still visible. This is situated at the junction of Buena Vista Drive and Plymbridge Road at SX 502609, not far from the George Hotel; here is a short length of the formation leading in a northerly direction, now appearing as a grassy and very overgrown lane.

Secondly, there was a formerly a large piece of dressed granite which lay beside the railway for many years on the southern side of the road to Clearbrook. It appeared to have fallen off a wagon en route from the quarries and was left where it fell. However, in 1981 a memorial was required to commemorate the wartime airfield at Yelverton Harrowbeer, and the stone was taken away by helicopter in order to form the memorial. It was then suitably inscribed and is now mounted very appropriately on a base composed of stone sleeper blocks near Leg O' Mutton corner at Yelverton (SX 518679).

The large piece of dressed granite retrieved from the side of the railway's course and inscribed to commemorate the wartime airfield at Yelverton Harrowbeer. Note the base composed of stone sleeper blocks.

Inside the industrial museum at Saltram House, Plympton. In front of the locomotive are examples of P. & D.R. stone sleeper blocks and early fish-bellied rails and chairs. Under the coupling of the locomotive are a cable roller and pulley from the Cann Wood incline of the Lee Moor Tramway.

It is fascinating to hear recollections of the Lee Moor Tramway's working days as told by persons who could remember it as part of their daily lives. The late Mr H. Nicholson related a story told by his father concerning the arrival of the steam locomotives in 1899. The general local opinion was that the wagons, having been used to horse haulage, would "never keep up with they engines"! Mr Nicholson also said that if two locomotives were in steam at the same time, and a particularly long and heavy train of clay had to be worked from Torycombe to Cann incline head, the second engine would give the train "a hefty push" from the rear. This would enable it to traverse the very sharp Wotter curve, and after that the leading engine could manage the load alone. He also remembered coal being brought up to Lee Moor on the tramway, unloaded at a wharf near the carpenters' shop in the village and then sold to local householders. On the Torycombe incline, bell signals were used between the upper and lower ends, the "right away" always being given from the lower end so as to ensure that the upward load had been attached!

Further memories came from Mrs. P. Rich, whose father, John Bray, was in charge of the southern terminus of the tramway at Martin's Wharf, together with the stabling of the horses that were used to haul the trains. She stated that during her childhood, around the time of World War I, her father would, on special occasions, clean out one of the tramway wagons and line it with straw or sacking. She and other members of the family would then journey on the tramway as far as Plym Bridge and, later, the 'passenger wagon' would form part of a train returning to Lee Moor, which sometimes included wagons of coal loaded from the GWR transfer sidings at Laira being taken up for the works and villagers. She clearly remembered the Lee Moor train waiting to cross the GWR line at Laira, and said that the horses (with names like 'Major' or 'Blucher') were not frightened by the passing of the main-line trains – although the children were!

Thirty six years after its final abandonment, remains of the system are gradually disappearing, but stone sleeper blocks mark the route in many places. In addition, both steam locomotives and a clay wagon are preserved, along with smaller relics such as lineside notices and examples of early rails and chairs.

The Museums at Saltram House in Devon and Wheal Martyn in Cornwall are open at certain times during the year, so that those interested are able to inspect these relics of a remarkable transport system. Hopefully, this will continue for many years to come.

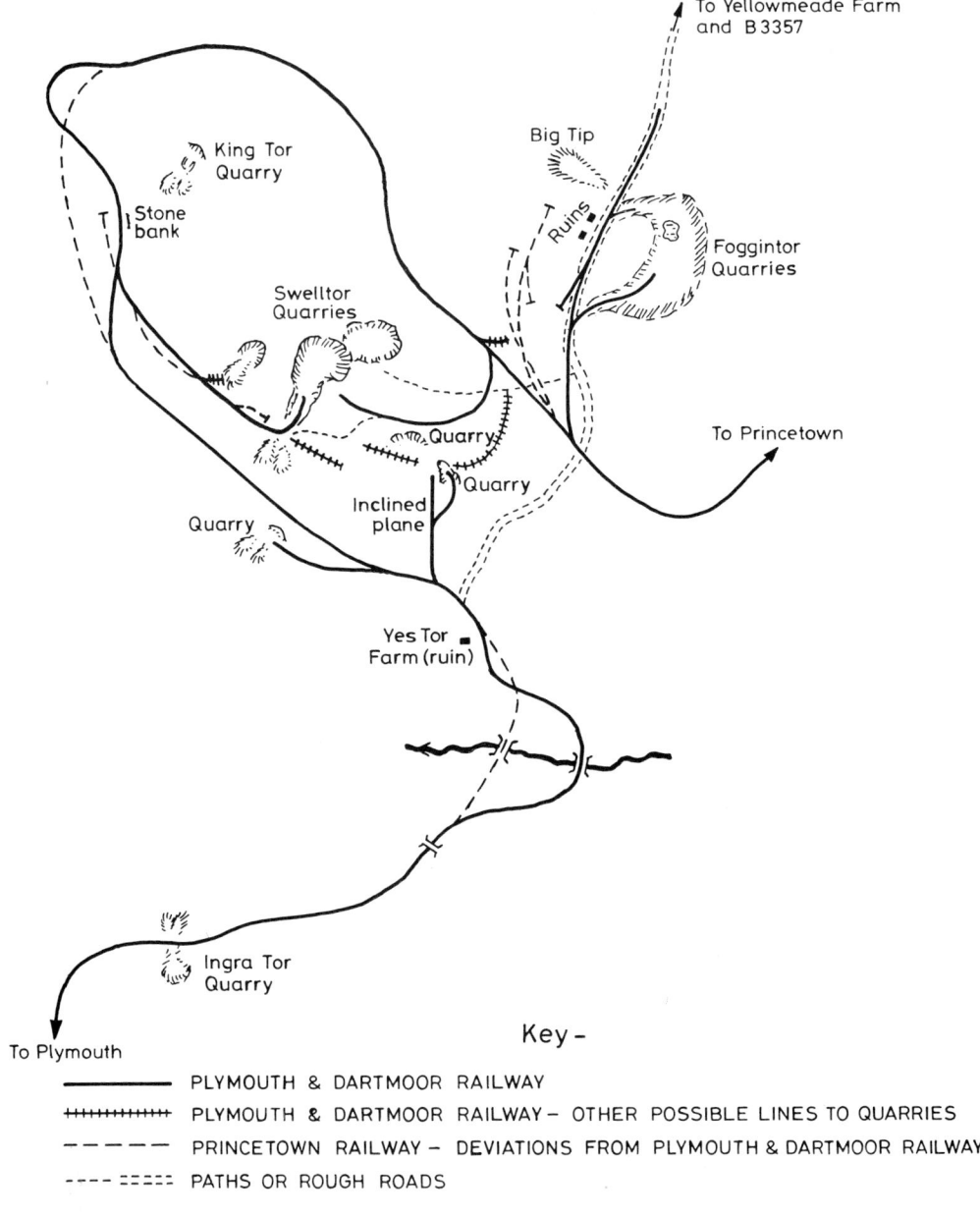

THE GRANITE QUARRIES OF WALKHAMPTON COMMON

(This chapter includes references only to remains from the period during which the Plymouth & Dartmoor Railway was in operation. Consequently later features, such as the massive stone corbels, which can now be seen near the Swelltor quarries, are not included)

Any exploration of the remains of the railway today must include the area of moorland on Walkhampton Common containing the granite quarries, which provided the major part of the traffic carried over the line. The two largest quarries were at Foggintor, sometimes known as Royal Oak (SX 567736), and at Swell Tor (SX 560733), whilst there were smaller workings at King Tor (SX 555738) and at Ingra Tor (SX 556721).

The lines of the Plymouth & Dartmoor Railway which served these quarries have been disused for over a century, and in some places it is now difficult to define precisely their former track-beds. This is particularly so in the vicinity of the Swelltor quarries, where the formation of the later standard-gauge sidings also exists, probably having been constructed directly on that of the original railway. What is certain, however, is the fact that over the years a considerable number of lines were constructed into, and around, the quarries in order to facilitate the removal of the granite.

When following the railway in the upward direction, the first quarry is found on the southern side of the line at Ingra Tor. It is approached through a narrow cutting, now partially filled with fallen rock, and two circular stone bases, which formerly supported cranes for loading the granite, can still be seen there. The waste tips from the excavation are situated on the opposite (northern) side of the track-bed of the 'main' railway.

Continuing towards Princetown, and soon after passing the ruins of Yes Tor Farm, a wide formation ascends on the northern side at SX 562729. This is the inclined plane which served part of the Swelltor quarries area, and which was mentioned by the Rev. E. A. Bray in his account written in 1831. He described it as "an inclined plane of great breadth on which were chains running upon rollers". Stone sleeper blocks can be found in places on the plane, together with a stone in the lower half which has four holes spaced over a distance of about 21 inches; this, perhaps, formed a base for one of the rollers for the chains mentioned in the Rev. Bray's notes.

It is now difficult to visualise which part of the quarry area the incline served, as it does not appear to provide direct access to any of the remaining railway formations at its upper end. However, a further point of interest can be found on the eastern side of the upper part of the plane, where more stone sleeper blocks remain in what is now very wet ground. These indicate that a siding led off the incline and continued up into a deep, narrow quarry, which is now partially flooded. It is also worth noting that the summit of the plane can more easily be reached from a line branching from the 'main' line on the other side of the great loop around King Tor, and which will be described later.

Returning to the base of the plane, if the 'main' line is followed for a further short distance to SX 560729 a gate is seen in the fencing on the southern side. This gives access to a formation which continues around the hillside below, but parallel to, the 'main' line and, after passing through a gate, leads to a small quarry. Here, on the northern side of the quarry, are the ruins of a small but substantial building. It is the stone sleeper blocks on the track-bed, though, that demand the attention for they show great variety, some with one, two, three or four holes drilled in them to receive the fixings for the rails.

On rejoining the 'main' line and following it towards Princetown, a stone bank can be seen on the eastern side of the formation at SX 554737. It is quite possible that this was a loading point serving the nearby King Tor quarry, which was a small working with no direct rail access. A narrow cutting can be seen leading from the quarry out onto tips on the hillside.

From near the stone bank just mentioned, a formation leads back along the hillside towards the Swelltor quarries, keeping parallel with the 'main' line, but at a higher level. The track-bed runs beside heaps of stone-cutters' waste and past a short, curving formation which diverges on the northern side into an overgrown cutting; this terminates beneath a waste tip and there is no clue as to its purpose. The line to the quarries, meanwhile, continues straight ahead and presently turns very sharply to the north-east up a deep and narrow cutting to reach the main quarry. On the opposite side, waste tips run out onto

A view of the main quarry at Swell Tor clearly showing the narrow cutting for the railway. Beyond the tips, and across the valley, can be seen Ingra Tor.

the hillside. Beyond this point, a well-defined formation continues through a shallow cutting, but ends abruptly on a stone embankment. It has been suggested that the original line to the quarry was laid in from this direction, but remains which can be seen now do not support this theory. A path leads from a point near the main Swelltor quarry to join another formation which passes near the top of the inclined plane, but it rises too steeply to have ever carried rails.

The Swelltor quarries were also served by one further branch of the railway, but this left the 'main' line some distance farther on, curving from the other arm of the great loop at SX 563734. The site of the junction lies on the western side, and from here the track-bed can be followed as it climbs upwards in a sweeping semi-circle. The formation is very clear, and numerous stone sleeper blocks remain on the upper portion. A study of the blocks will show the method of construction of the line; a sleeper block will be seen with four holes drilled to receive the fixing for a rail (or chair), the next block has no holes and was presumably just placed as a support, whilst the third has two holes. Similarly, the fourth has no holes, the fifth has two, the sixth none and the seventh again has four. This sequence is then repeated, each section being a few inches over 16 feet in length.

The track-bed continues, passing above the summit of the inclined plane and between tips of waste stone, almost to the lip of the main quarry. At this point it reaches a height of some 1,250 feet above sea-level, this being 100 feet above the line described previously, which entered the quarry at its lower end. To the north is a further excavation of the quarry, which is at a higher level and has no clear point of access, except into the main quarry below. Another route leading into the Swell Tor area is a wide path that follows the hillside parallel with, but below, the line described in the preceding paragraph. It has no sleeper blocks and the lower end terminates at the footpath linking the Foggintor and Swell Tor areas, but it has the appearance of being the track-bed of a former railway. The line would have entered the quarries near the summit of the inclined plane, although immediately before reaching that point it is severed by the excavation of the deep and partially flooded quarry which was served from the plane, as previously mentioned. Beyond this quarry lies the summit of the plane, a small flat area with another quarry behind it, whilst beyond again, a path, which could be a continuation of the formation, extends for some distance along the hillside. Whether this route was part of the railway system is not clear but, if it was, it must have been abandoned before the deep and partially flooded quarry was being worked to its full extent.

The final quarry connected to the railway is situated at Foggintor and, like Ingra Tor, lies outside the great loop of the line around King's Tor. The junction of its branch line, at SX 565732, is very near to the site of the later King Tor Halt of the GWR, and the track-bed, rather indistinct at first, runs roughly parallel to the stony track coming up from the ruined Yes Tor Farm. It crosses the path leading to Swell Tor and follows a shallow, rush-filled

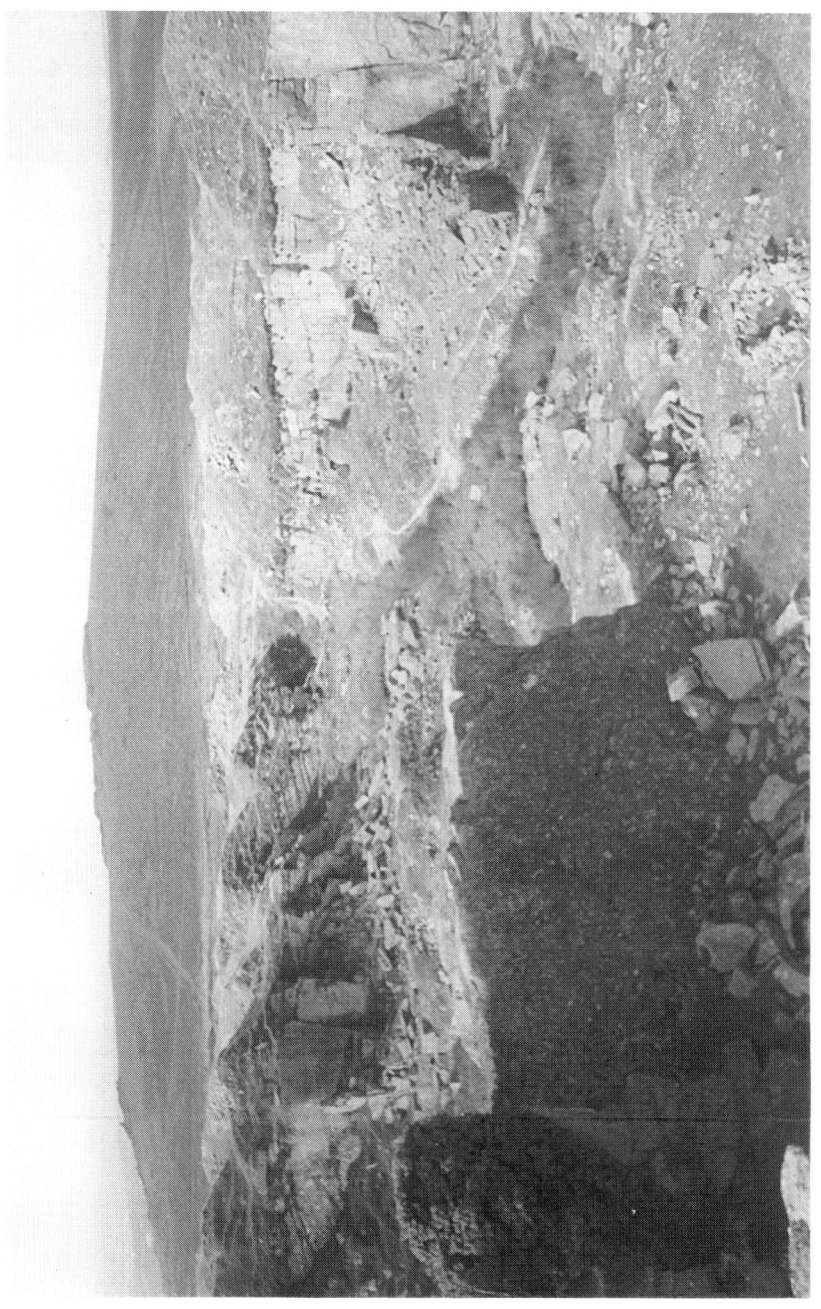

A view of the southern portion of Foggintor Quarry showing, in the centre of the picture, the point of entry of the railway. The Swelltor quarries lie on the far side of the hill in the background.

depression with a low stone bank on the eastern side before merging with the stony track; here stone sleeper blocks may be seen. Here, too, more sleeper blocks indicate that a branch line led off eastwards through a (now wet) cutting into the main part of Foggintor Quarry, itself, where stone bases for cranes may still be seen. It is a very large excavation and contains a considerable sheet of water. Also, at the point of junction, further sleeper blocks suggest that yet another line ran westwards from the quarry towards the tips of waste stone.

Following the stony track northwards, further sleeper blocks are visible (with some breaks) leading past a siding on the western side and, a little later, a curving, rush-filled depression on the eastern side. This was almost certainly a second branch leading into the higher part of the quarry, although no sleeper blocks are to be seen there. The ruins of former dwellings lie on the western side of the track, together with several tips of waste stone; these include one very large heap, known locally as 'Big Tip', which stretches for a considerable distance in a north-westerly direction. Beyond the ruins and tips, the stone sleeper blocks may be traced for some distance along the track leading towards Yellowmeade Farm.

There is one other short formation which appears to have been constructed to carry rails, this being a short curving length leaving the 'main line' at SX 563734. It ends abruptly at the point where it reaches the site of the Royal Oak siding of the GWR, on the other side of which there is no sign of any continuation towards the quarry.

Such are the remains of the railway to be seen around the quarries today, and no doubt further lines were laid out onto the numerous waste tips.

Note: The sites of the various quarries have many features of interest for those interested in railways or industrial archaeology. In addition, there are magnificent views over the surrounding countryside. It must be remembered, however, that the quarry excavations are unfenced and that some parts of the ground are very uneven. Consequently, any exploration must be undertaken with due care at all times.

APPENDICES

Appendix I – Relics in Preservation

In addition to the visible remains along the various routes of the railways, the following relics survive in preservation:–

1. In the Lee Moor Tramway Museum at Saltram House, Plympton.

    'LEE MOOR No 2' Peckett 0–4–0 saddle tank locomotive.
    Rebuilt truck (numbered 44).
    Signal from the level-crossing over the main railway line from Paddington at Laira.
    Wooden cab backplate formerly fitted to locomotive.
    Incline pulley and box from Cann Wood.
    Incline roller from Cann Wood
    Short length of winding cable from Cann Wood.
    Several pieces of early butt-jointed and lap-jointed rails, with stone sleeper blocks.
    Large scale map of the Lee Moor system.
    Track gauge used on the tramway.

2. In the Wheal Martyn China Clay Museum at Carthew, near St Austell.

    'LEE MOOR No 1' Peckett 0–4–0 saddle tank locomotive.
    Restored signal box from Torycombe level-crossing, Lee Moor Tramway.
    Notice from Cann Wood incline regarding maximum loads.

Appendix II – Distances (mileage of lines)

	Miles
Sutton Pool – Yelverton – Princetown.	$25\frac{1}{2}$
Cattewater (Martin's Quay) branch.	$0\frac{1}{4}$
Crabtree – Marsh Mills.	$0\frac{1}{2}$
Marsh Mills – Cann Quarry.	2
Marsh Mills – Plympton.	1
Plym Bridge – Lee Moor – Cholwichtown.	5
Wotter branch.	$0\frac{1}{2}$
The Lee Moor Tramway from Cattewater (Martin's Quay) to Cholwichtown, incorporating parts of above routes.	$8\frac{1}{2}$

Appendix III – Inscription on the stone commemorating Harrowbeer Airfield

R.A.F. Harrowbeer operational 1941–1949

From this station flew pilots of many Commonwealth and Allied Countries including Britain, Canada, Czecho-Slovakia, France, Poland, Rhodesia and the United States of America with the support of their ground crew and air defence units.

This stone in memory of all who served here and especially of those who gave their lives.

Many local residents helped build and maintain this airfield.

Unveiled by the first station commander, Group Captain the Honourable E. F. Ward. on 15th August 1981 the fortieth anniversary of the opening of this station.

Appendix IV – Chronology

1818	(3rd November) First proposal for railway by Sir Thomas Tyrwhitt.
1819	(2nd July) Act of Incorporation of Plymouth & Dartmoor Railway Company.
1819	(12th August) First rail laid by Sir Thomas.
1820	(8th July) Act for extension to Sutton Pool.
1821	(2nd July) Act for deviation via Leigham Tunnel.
1823	(26th September) Railway opened from Crabtree to King Tor.
1825	(December) Extension to Sutton Pool completed.
1826	(December) Extension to Princetown completed.
1829	(November) Branch to Marsh Mills completed.
1833	Branch to Marsh Mills extended to Cann Quarry.
1834	Branch to Plympton completed.
1847	Branch to Plympton purchased by South Devon Railway, and closed.
1851	(23rd April) Sutton Pool branch purchased by South Devon Railway.
1853/4	Construction, trial working and suspension of traffic on Lee Moor Tramway.
1855	Regular traffic ceased on Cann Quarry branch.
1857	Sutton Pool branch converted to mixed 4ft. 6in. and 7ft. 0¼in. gauges.
1858	(24th September) Lee Moor Tramway officially re-opened.
1865	Plymouth & Dartmoor Railway Company reconstituted.
1869	(19th April) Locomotive haulage introduced on Sutton Pool branch, and 4ft. 6in. gauge line removed.

113

1875	(19th July) Act for Branch to Cattewater to be worked by L & SWR.
1878	Wotter viaduct replaced by route around valley.
1878	(13th August) Act for construction of Great Western Railway branch to Princetown, and rebuilding of most of Plymouth & Dartmoor Railway route above Yelverton.
1883	(2nd August) Act for branch to Turnchapel to be worked by L & SWR.
1888	(28th June) Act for branch from Plymstock to Yealmpton, to be worked by GWR.
1899	Steam locomotives introduced on part of Lee Moor Tramway.
1900	Wotter branch closed to traffic.
1916	Rails lifted from Cann Quarry branch beyond Plym Bridge and from Plymouth & Dartmoor Railway between Yelverton and Crabtree.
1921	Plymouth & Dartmoor Railway absorbed into group of companies forming Southern Railway.
1933	Line to Cholwichtown closed to traffic.
1936	Line from Torycombe to Lee Moor village closed to traffic.
1945	(31st December) Lee Moor Tramway closed to regular traffic.
1960	(26th August) Sand trains on lower part of Lee Moor Tramway withdrawn, and tramway abandoned.
1964	Formation of Lee Moor Tramway Preservation Society.
1970	(20th July) Restored 'Lee Moor No 2' removed to Museum at Saltram, Plympton.
1975	(17th March) Restored 'Lee Moor No 1' removed to Wheal Martyn Museum, St Austell.

BIBLIOGRAPHY

Crossing's Dartmoor Worker, W. Crossing (David & Charles, 1966)

Dartmoor, R. Hansford Worth (David & Charles, 1967)

Dartmoor – A New Study, various authors (David & Charles, 1977)

Industrial Archaeology of Dartmoor, H. Harris (David & Charles, 1968)

Map of the Plymouth & Dartmoor Railway (southern section) and the Lee Moor Tramway, R. C. Sambourne and J. C. Gillham (1965)

Mineral Railways of the Westcountry, Fairclough/Shepherd (Bradford Barton, 1975)

The Canals of South West England, C. Hadfield (David & Charles, 1967)

The Lee Moor Tramway, B. Gibson (Plymouth Railway Circle, 1993)

The Lee Moor Tramway, R. M. S. Hall, M.A. (Oakwood Press, 1963)

The Lee Moor Tramway, W. O. Meade King (Extract from *ECC Review*, 1961)

The Plymouth & Dartmoor Railway, H. G. Kendall (Oakwood Press, 1968)

The Railway Magazine – Dec 1908, Mar 1934, Oct 1940, Nov 1964 and Apr 1969

The Tavistock, Launceston & Princetown Railways, G. H. Anthony, M.C.I.T. (Oakwood Press, 1971)

The Yelverton to Princetown Railway, A. R. Kingdom (Forest Publishing, 1991)

Transactions of the Devonshire Association – 1905 and 1908

Walking the Dartmoor Railroads, E. Hemery (David & Charles, 1983)

THE AUTHOR

Eric Shepherd was born in Torquay in 1924. After being educated at the local Grammar School, he commenced training as a Sanitary Inspector prior to serving for 3 years with the Royal Engineers in England and Egypt. Following demobilisation, he completed his training and was appointed to a position with a Rural District Council near Southend-on-Sea in Essex, where he remained for 4 years. During this period Eric also took the opportunity to visit some East Anglian railways.

After marrying and returning to Devon, Eric's career with Local Government continued until retirement, since when he has been able to devote more time to leisure activities. He still lives near Plymouth with his wife, Margaret, and they have a daughter Anne, who holds an executive position with the Department of the Environment in London.

Railways have always been Eric's great interest and boyhood memories include Saturday morning trips on branch lines near his home town, as well as many hours spent sitting on the wall by Newton Abbot station watching the passing trains and also the locomotives running to and from the sheds there. Another favourite, and frequently visited, location was near the signal box at Dainton summit, which had the added advantage of providing an opportunity to see the banking locomotives waiting to return to either Totnes or Newton Abbot. A particularly nostalgic memory of Eric's is of two trips over the Lynton & Barnstaple Railway during the final few weeks of its existence in 1935.

He is a member of several railway preservation societies and his other interests include Church organ playing and walking on Dartmoor.

Eric R. Shepherd